Earl's Pearls

Earl's Pearls

Jewels of Wisdom Worth Passing On

Earl Heard and Brady Porche

BIC Publishing

BIC Publishing
P. O. Box 40166
Baton Rouge, LA 70835-0166
(800) 460-4242
www.bicalliance.com

Earl's Pearls

First Printing

Printed in the United States of America

ISBN: 978-0-9768310-5-1

Printed by RR Donnelley
Crawfordsville, IN
Cover design and layout by
Denise Simoneaux & Heather Abboud

Quantity discounts available. Dealer inquiries welcome.

This book is dedicated to a loving and forgiving God, who has given me and many others the strength to overcome adversity through faith, hard work and perseverance. This book is also dedicated to those who have played a role in bringing peace, happiness and success to others by sharing their life lessons and experiences.

I would like to give thanks to my wife Bodi, my daughter Dane, my son-in-law and partner Thomas Brinsko, and my wonderful grandchildren — Hannah, Mary and Michael — for inspiring me to be a better person. A special thanks to my family, friends and BIC Alliance partners, along with everyone who has used the services of BIC Alliance, IVS Investment Banking and BIC Recruiting, for without you we would not have the information or resources to publish BIC Magazine, Earl's Pearls or any of our other books.

I would like to extend my deepest gratitude to Rick Phillips, Whitney Strickland, Connie Voss, Shirley White and Scott Whitelaw for supplying us with some of the best information on motivation, leadership, professional development and sales and marketing I've ever read. We consider it an honor to have such talented and experienced individuals share their expertise in the pages of BIC Magazine and Earl's Pearls.

I would like to thank Brady Porche for his dedication in selecting and editing the best of the best articles in the aforementioned categories and coordinating with the authors at every stage. I thank our cover design and layout team of Heather Abboud and Denise Simoneaux for creating yet another fine product to share with the world. I would also like to thank the BIC Magazine editors — Kaye Benham, Anna Matherne and Jennifer Berthelot — for their help in proof-reading and editing the text. Special thanks go to Jairo Alvarez, Mark Hertzog, Thomas Turner, Michelle Holyfield, Brian Kinchen, Lynda Broussard and Collin Wimberly for reviewing the book before it went to press and providing us with their kind remarks.

Last but certainly not least, I would like to thank everyone who submitted proverbs and Bible verses to be included in this book — Dawn Beamon, Kaye Benham, Thomas and Dane Brinsko, John Bird, Bill Brossart, Kevin and Kim Browning, Dave Fanta, Terry Grover, Kim Heard, Mary Alice "Bodi" Heard, Mark Hertzog, Buz Lowry, Rick Phillips, Darren Tidwell, Bruce Wesley and Shirley White.

Earl B Heard

Earl Heard

Praise for Earl's Pearls

"Great job on this collection! I feel that you have included a perfect variety of topics — although not everyone may be interested in each topic, there is certainly a topic that everyone will have interest in."

Michelle Holyfield, Responsible Care® Coordinator, Eastman Chemical Co.

"Earl's Pearls offers sound advice that will improve anyone's ability to succeed in life!"

Thomas Turner, COO/Vice Chairman, Turner Industries

"Women often wear pearls around their necks, but these are the kind of pearls that everyone should wear in their hearts."

Brian Kinchen, Member of the 2003 World Champion New England Patriots, Head Football Coach of Ascension Christian High School (La.)

"When I was reading Earl's Pearls I thought of the words of Andy Rooney: 'There is more to know than we have time to learn. I think civilization suffers from lack of knowledge.' This book fills humanity's need for knowledge because it is the summary of many, many years of experience, covering the triumphs and tribulations of the authors. Earl's Pearls should be read by people of all walks of life, with no distinction for religion, race or origin."

Jairo Alvarez-Botero, President, Alvarez Construction Co.

"Right from page 1, Earl's Pearls takes you on a jet ride to self-improvement in your business, personal and spiritual journeys that will leave you changed ... and charged to create and tackle the next new exciting phase in your life.

Whether you work in the energy sector or some other industry or business, you will benefit from these gems. And whether you plan to read Earl's Pearls in a single sitting, or you are going to dig up its jewels over several expeditions, buckle your seatbelt. Get your highlighter and pen and notebook ready — you're going on a treasure hunt!"

Mark S. Hertzog, President, 2020 Media LLC

"Earl's Pearls is a treasure! Filled with wit, wisdom, and biblical insight, it is a joy to read. I wholeheartedly recommend it!"

Dr. Collin Wimberly, Pastor, Parkview Baptist Church (Baton Rouge, La.)

"Being in the event planning business for a number of years, I've seen firsthand many advantages that can result from the professional networking strategies described in Earl's Pearls."

Lynda Broussard, President, Broussard Advertising

Contents

About the Authors

Earl Heard

Earl Heard is the founder and CEO of the Business and Industry Communications (BIC) Alliance, a multi-industry strategic marketing firm; IVS Investment Banking, a merger-and-acquisition and investment banking firm; BIC Recruiting, an executive recruiting firm; and BIC Media Solutions, a custom publishing, event planning and management and sales training company. He is the publisher of *BIC Magazine*, the Western Hemisphere's largest multi-industry, multidepartmental energy, construction and environmental publication. His Alligator Management & Marketing seminars and keynote presentations are delivered on a regular basis to sales and management professionals in business and industry.

A former manager with both Ethyl Corp. and Hill Petroleum, Heard has garnered extensive experience in operations, fire and safety, human resources, training, public relations, employee relations, and personnel as a hands-on member of industry.

He is also the author of the 2005 book, *It's What We Do Together That Counts: The BIC Alliance Story*, in which he explains how through faith, hard work and perseverance, we can achieve greater peace, happiness and success in our lives. BIC Media Solutions, through its BIC Publishing division, released *Energy Entrepreneurs*, a compilation of stories about successful entrepreneurs in the energy industry in 2007, followed by *Industry Achievers*, a collection of life lessons shared by leaders in business and industry, in 2009.

Heard lives in Baton Rouge, La., with his wife, Mary "Bodi" Heard.

1

Thomas Brinsko

Previously an attorney for Exxon and Key Production, Thomas Brinsko joined BIC Alliance and IVS Investment Banking in 1999 and became president and COO in 2002.

His industrial background and his business development, legal and acquisition experience has given him the ability to match buyers' and sellers' complementary capabilities, values and vision. Along with fellow managing partners, he has completed numerous investment banking transactions and created hundreds of strategic industrial marketing plans and campaigns.

Brinsko received an undergraduate degree in business from the University of Southwestern Louisiana (now the University of Louisiana-Lafayette) and a juris doctorate from Louisiana State University's Paul M. Hebert Law Center. His active participation in various associations related to the petrochemical and refining industries includes a seat on the board of the Association of Chemical Industry of Texas and a leadership role in the Christian Refining and Petrochemical Fellowship.

Brinsko lives in Houston with his wife Dane and their three children — Hannah, Mary and Michael.

Rick Phillips

Rick Phillips founded Phillips Sales and Staff Development in 1984 and today his work is recognized by his peers. He serves as a consultant to clients in industries ranging from food service and hospitality to energy, insurance and academia. In 2009, he joined BIC Alliance as a sales and management training consultant.

Phillips has been a featured speaker at the international convention for the American Society for Training and Development (ASTD). He is a past winner of the ASTD Training Program Design Award, and he has received Toastmasters International's highest earned honor — being named Distinguished Toastmaster — and was a featured presenter at their international convention. As a member of the National Speakers Association, Phillips served as president of the organization's Louisiana chapter, spoke at their international convention and has been named Chapter Member of the Year.

Phillips has also served on the board of directors of organizations in Louisiana and Texas and was a founding board member of The International Center for Customer Service Studies. He sat on the board of the Center for Effective Leadership, a group of internationally recognized consultants, pooling their talents to increase individual effectiveness for clients. He earned his bachelor's degree from Chaminade University of Honolulu and his master's degree from Central Michigan University with studies at Georgetown University.

Whitney Strickland

Whitney Strickland is the vice president and chief marketing officer for the turn-around and maintenance company AltairStrickland. Strickland has been working in various capacities within the refining, chemical, petrochemical, fertilizer, pulp and paper, and power industries for most of his 25-year career. He literally started at the bottom cleaning tanks, then advanced to become a pipefitter and a welder and performed other crafts as his skills grew. This "bottom-up" experience has given Strickland a valuable opportunity to understand the physical aspects of a production facility. It also allowed him to forge good working relationships with labor, management, staff and clients.

Strickland's background in technology and Web-based tools was also an advantage. He later became a project staffing director, filling as many as 1,000 job slots for a single project, often within 24 hours' notice. He advanced to estimating and then on to sales, ultimately assuming his current position, where he applied his skills and knowledge to help grow the business from $40 million to over $240 million annual gross sales.

Strickland is also a board member and supporter of The Wheelhouse Inc., a Deer Park, Texas-based program that helps men recover from alcoholism and drug addiction through spirituality. He and his wife Tisha have three children — Aubrey, Angus and Christopher.

Connie Voss

Connie Voss is the owner of Voss & Associates, a full-service advertising agency and marketing consulting firm located in Houston. Her clients sell to the refining, chemical, petrochemical, pulp and paper, marine, HVAC and power industries. She helps them market their products and/or services through an integrated program of sales tools and marketing planning.

"After college I quickly learned that a BA only served as a launching pad to my career because markets are dynamic, not static, therefore the learning never stops," says Voss. "I am fortunate to have gained the ability to merge experience, creativity and persuasion into a unique selling message for our clients then place that message in the appropriate media and make it stick. Helping our clients gain market share is what we are all about."

She has received numerous awards for her work, including three for a coffee-table book she researched, wrote and produced that recounted the 100-year history of a private boys' school. She also ghostwrites articles and books for select businesspeople.

Shirley A. White, MBA, EdD, CCC

"Helping others to achieve a winning edge" is the mission of Shirley White, founder of Success Images, a career coaching and communications consulting firm. Dr. White is a certified career coach, workshop leader, consultant and author. She is also a columnist — her guest articles on self-improvement and career issues have been published in *BIC Magazine* on a regular basis for more than 20 years. In addition, Dr. White is a contributor to the book, *Dear Success Seeker: Wisdom from Outstanding Women Achievers*, with foreword written by Dr. Camille Cosby. She is the author of the quick and easy-to-read *101 Winning Tips for Getting a Job* and *Dress to Win: 10 Steps to Maximum Personal Impact*.

Dr. White worked in academia as a management professor in the Louisiana State University College of Business Administration for 12 years. She also taught business classes for seven years in the community college setting in Chicago and Phoenix. Additionally, Dr. White has worked as a training facilitator with the State of Louisiana's Comprehensive Public Training Program. She used her experience in interpersonal communications as a consultant with the LSU Cox Communications Academic Center for Student-Athletes, where she conducted media training for all of the teams.

For more than 25 years, Dr. White has been providing a variety of career coaching services for a diverse clientele. Drawing on her extensive background, she brings a wealth of knowledge and expertise to her clients. Her enthusiasm, talent and commitment add to her ability to help others unlock their potential to achieve a winning edge for career and life success.

A native of Chicago and a resident of Baton Rouge, Dr. White has three children and eight grandchildren.

Scott Whitelaw

Scott Whitelaw is an environmental, health and safety professional with 28 years of operational and management experience. Whitelaw began his career in Louisiana as a contract employee working on oil and gas offshore rigs, progressing quickly into a management position in an oil field service company working and living in Southeast Asia. Upon returning to the United States, Whitelaw entered graduate school, earning an MBA from the University of Denver. Upon graduation, he was selected to Conoco's prestigious management development program. Whitelaw had a 10-year career with Conoco, working in various oil and gas upstream, downstream and transportation areas in Colorado, Texas, Virginia and Wyoming. For the past 14 years, he has been in the hydrocarbon storage, solution mining and salt business, responsible for environmental, health, safety and regulatory and governmental affairs for Texas United Corp. with operations in Texas, Louisiana, New Mexico, Virginia and New York.

Whitelaw holds a bachelor of science degree in environmental science from Florida Institute of Technology and an MBA with an emphasis in energy management from the University of Denver. Over the course of his career, he has been active in numerous local, state and national committees addressing emergency, environmental and safety issues. He is a frequent speaker for various organizations, companies and conferences, including the National Safety Council, Texas Chemical Council and American Chemistry Council.

Growing up as an Army brat and working in the oil and gas business provided Whitelaw the geographical and cultural experiences of living in 10 different U.S. states and four foreign countries. Whitelaw and his wife Lynne reside in Spring, Texas, and have two children. Both kids are attending college; daughter Tori attends Texas A&M and son Bo is a student at Virginia Tech.

About the Editor

Brady Porche

Brady Porche is the senior editor of *BIC Magazine*. Over the course of his career, he has interviewed and written feature articles about executives, managers and entrepreneurs in a variety of industries, including petrochemical, construction, specialty contracting, tourism, hospitality, professional sports and more. He co-edited Earl Heard's first book, *It's What We Do Together That Counts: The BIC Alliance Story*, in 2005, and co-wrote with Heard *Energy Entrepreneurs* (2007) and *Industry Achievers* (2009).

Preface

Dear friends,

My mission for this book is to help everyone who reads it to find greater peace, happiness and success here on earth — whether it's on the job or at home — and eternal life in Heaven. I'm praying that this book touches the lives of folks who have never heard of BIC Alliance and even total strangers who don't know God and may not even have much love for Americans or even their own families or fellow man. In our company and in our family, our mission is to use our resources to connect people in business, industry and the community with one another for the betterment of all. *Earl's Pearls* is the latest part of that endeavor.

I'm also praying that those of you who are people of faith and who have already found peace, happiness and success in your life will pray for the success of this book in touching others. I'm praying that all who read this book, even those who are not people of faith, are moved to share its passages with others you love and care about and even strangers whom you think may benefit from one of the "pearls" you enjoyed most.

In preparation for each section of the book Brady Porche and I have spent many hours reviewing guest articles that have run in *BIC Magazine* over the years to select the best of the best in the following four areas — motivation, leadership, professional development, and sales and marketing. While it isn't possible to develop a how-to manual containing solutions to all of the challenges we face in our professional lives, we believe this anthology of sorts contains just as many helpful hints, technical tips and life lessons as any similar volume on bookshelves today.

As for the ensuing section, which includes ages-old proverbs and Bible verses, we requested input from our families, friends, BIC Alliance colleagues and readers of *BIC Magazine*. Out of several hundred proverbs we reviewed, we have chosen about 100 that we believe will be memorable and serve as food for thought. As for our Biblical section, in addition to soliciting favorite verses and passages from family, friends and fellow BICsters I've read the Bible and other faith related books more in the past six months than I have since taking Bible classes at Louisiana College in the early 1960s.

The more I read and reread the Bible the more thankful I became that some members of my family, friends, co-workers and other people of faith didn't give up on me when I was not truly born again. In my reading of the Bible, I was comforted when I read that even among the 12 disciples of Jesus there were times when they fell asleep and either denied Jesus or doubted him. Not only did one of the 12, Judas, betray Jesus, but Peter — one of the closest to Jesus — denied knowing him three times in less than 24 hours. Another close disciple, Thomas, doubted Jesus' rebirth so strongly that he had to see the messiah's nail-scarred hands before believing. If those closest to Jesus were not perfect, then that should be a great lesson for all of us. Even though none of us is perfect we can still strive for perfection not only in our walk with God

9

but in our relationships here on earth.

There was a time when I had fallen as far away from God as anyone can be. Even in those times (and even today) I know that family members like my wife Bodi, who is also a reborn Christian; my daughter Dane and son-in-law Thomas Brinsko; my dearly departed mother and father, Margie and Leo Heard; my late sister-in-law Beverly; my mother-in-law Yvonne Bodi; and my fellow BICsters and friends like pastor Charles "Peanut" Hull, Bob Hornsby, Claude Barber, David Starkey and others (some who I don't even know) continued to pray for me when I wasn't even praying for myself. Even today I welcome your prayers that the work we are doing individually and together through BIC Alliance will touch the lives of others for the better.

To me, the key to finding peace, happiness and success lies in being able to look toward the heavens and into our hearts and into the eyes of those we love and care about and even the unlovable and to know without a shadow of doubt that we're doing our best to share our faith and follow the golden rule with others.

When I became born again and began doing unto others as I would have them do unto me my whole world changed for the better. In closing I feel that I would be remiss in my duty to God, those I care and our fellow mankind if I failed to share this message. If you are already saved and your life is full of peace, happiness and success I encourage you to join me in sharing your blessings and life lessons with others.

In the weeks before we sent this book off to the press, our beloved New Orleans Saints won Super Bowl XLIV. The positive global media coverage surrounding the Saints and their relationship with their home city and state and the Gulf Coast region after years of devastating natural disasters proved that the world is hungry to hear stories of people overcoming adversity through hard work, faith and perseverance. As my friend Jairo Alvarez, president of Alvarez Construction, says, there is no such thing as impossible.

All we have to do is recall the image of Saints quarterback and Super Bowl MVP Drew Brees holding his son toward the heavens in the moments following the game and we'll know that there are no greater feelings than the love of God and family and, of course, being a winner in your chosen field of endeavor. The "Who Dat" nation believes that faith and destiny played a part in the rebirth of the Saints and the Gulf Coast region, and the Super Bowl victory has helped inspire hope and greater love for a city, state and region that many of us already knew was a great place to live and visit. Just as the Saints' story inspired that feeling, I'm praying that the guest articles, proverbs and verses featured in *Earl's Pearls* will help inspire greater faith, hope, love of mankind and self-worth for those who read it. Many of these jewels of wisdom have changed my life, just as they have changed the lives of those who contributed to this book. I'm sure they will do the same for you.

May God bless you, your family and your endeavors,

Earl B. Heard
CEO & Founder
BIC Alliance

Introduction

Business/motivational books are aplenty these days. Surely the glut of printed matter about how to succeed in business is a sign that the market for it is alive and well. What role the recent recession has played in that dynamic is to be debated only by publishing industry analysts and economic gurus.

With so many great business and motivational books, with their promises to teach readers the habits of highly effective people, train them in the art of "thinking without thinking" or show them how to make the metaphysical transition from "good" to "great" flying off the shelves, where does *Earl's Pearls* fit into the picture?

Some books tout easy answers, others claim to hold the keys to changing our lives in irrevocably positive ways. Personally, I believe this book is unique in its fusion of ideas and practices that can be easily imported into our everyday lives with others that take years of practice and wholesale commitment to perfect. Certainly, each of the individuals who penned these articles has enough experience to assist us in orienting our minds so that we can recognize these "jewels" when the light of day hits them and know how to apply them in the most effective ways.

I am proud of the fact that anyone who picks this book up can learn from Scott Whitelaw how to live life more passionately and overcome negative thinking, then turn a few pages and read Dr. Shirley White's essential rules for professional dress and dining etiquette. Likewise, you can read Earl Heard's thoughts on applying "The People Secret" or playing the game of life or Connie Voss's discussion of the effect of happiness on productivity and then learn how to give great presentations and enhance customer relations with sales and marketing experts like Whitney Strickland and Rick Phillips. If you are of the belief that there is a gravity imbalance between any of these life lessons, there are many successful business and industry executives who would likely say otherwise.

Although this is BIC Publishing's first anthology of guest articles, it fits nicely into the overall objective we envisioned when we began writing books back in 2004. The common thread among successful people is most of them have great stories to tell and useful knowledge to pass on to others. In our role as a company whose mission is "to connect people in business, industry and the community with one another for the betterment of all," we at BIC Alliance are often fortunate enough to have unparalleled access to such individuals. It is our hope that, through this book and those that will follow, we'll continue to inspire people young and old to adopt the "best practices" that have allowed ordinary people to achieve extraordinary things for generations.

Even with so much wisdom packed into this volume, I am sure that anyone who reads this book will have pearls of his own that are worth passing on. If so, share them with others and share them with us. We just might find a place for them in our next book.

Brady Porche
Baton Rouge, La.

How to Read and Retain Information More Effectively

(Heard)

Before you begin reading, here are some interesting facts and helpful hints about reading and retaining information.

- The average brain weighs about 3 lbs. and has about 10 billion cells. Most of us only use a fraction of our brains — about 10 percent.
- To improve memory, we only need to use more of our mental capacity.
- Memory can improve drastically by developing a system.
- We must be mentally ready, interested and motivated to learn better and faster.
- Repetition is usually the foundation for improving our reading and memory capacity.
- The average human brain can store about half a million pages of information, or several hundred large books.
- A positive mental attitude enables us to be more receptive to learning.
- People remember more when they are interested and the information is helpful.

Our job as publishers, writers and designers is to help make our magazine articles and our books more interesting and helpful.

- Job related and meaningful information is nine times easier to remember than meaningless information.
- Creating our own system of remembering works very well. Pride alone will help us read and remember better.
- The better we can plant information in our subconscious the better we will remember.
- Spaced learning is about 12-15 percent more effective than crammed learning.
- Experts agree that we do better by rewarding ourselves. By taking a break for a cup of coffee or a snack we are not only taking a physical break but also allowing our subconscious to review the material.
- By reading and saying something instead of just reading it, we can recall twice as much four hours later.
- By previewing and looking for key facts and ideas, a reader will retain

13

more. In magazines we use headlines, pictures, graphics and drop quotes to help capture and retain interest.

• The best way I know for reading and retaining more information is by reading with a highlighter, pad and pen nearby. I highlight key points I want to remember in each chapter then try to write down the key points in the margin or at the end of the chapter before proceeding. After finishing a book I always like to write a summary and then review the book periodically. A good article and a good book are like a good movie. We can enjoy them over and over for decades and share them with others.

It is important to remember that there are many rewards that come from learning, whether it is from a book, a magazine, a seminar, a DVD, a mentor or a personal experience. Not only can our rewards be emotional, personal and financial, we will have a better life when we know how to learn things easier. The "pearls" we share with you will work off the job as well as on. I believe if you take these pearls to heart and practice them daily you will have more peace, happiness, friends, success and respect from others and feel better about yourself.

Part I:

Motivation

*"We are all inventors, each sailing out on a
voyage of discovery, guided each by a private
chart, of which there is no duplicate.
The world is all gates, all opportunities."*

— Ralph Waldo Emerson

Failing Forward

(Whitelaw)

"Failure is merely an opportunity to intelligently begin again." — Henry Ford

Have you ever failed at something? Have you ever made a mistake? Have you ever feared your failures and criticized yourself for your mistakes? Have you ever avoided doing something because of the risk of failure? Have you ever let a mistake or failure cost you dearly in terms of money, health, career and/or relationships? If you have, it may be time to try a different strategy. "Failing forward" is a process of accepting responsibility for a failure and adopting a learning attitude for the purpose of moving forward — regardless of the consequences of any adverse outcome.

As an environmental and safety professional, I investigate industrial mistakes for a living. In many incident cases, the benefits derived from learning what caused the failure outweigh the costs and consequences of the incident. Every failure tells a story. If we understand and learn from failures, we can avoid and/or reduce any significant consequences from such unfortunate, costly failures. As an industrial professional, I was trained to succeed, but perhaps I should also have been trained to fail.

Do you remember the law of cause and effect? The Greek philosopher Aristotle came up with this idea in about 350 B.C. The law says that for every effect in your life, there are specific causes. Everything happens for a reason. Success is not an accident. Failure is not an accident. Failure takes work, as does success. Some people say it takes more work to fail than to succeed.

"Defeat, like a headache, warns us that something has gone wrong. If we are intelligent, we look for the cause and profit by the experience." — Napoleon Hill

People think that failure is avoidable; it is not. No human or system is perfect! Everyone makes mistakes. I think of mistakes as lessons that serve as fuel for the engine that drives continuous improvement. Learning from our failures allows us to achieve greater understanding, which will actually drive us toward higher challenges. It is OK to fail. If we are not failing, we are not growing. Our perseverance to hang tough through the repeated process of turning failure into improvement allows us to keep moving forward.

In his book, *Failing Forward*, John C. Maxwell describes seven abilities needed to fail forward:

1. Achievers reject rejection.
2. Achievers see failure as temporary.
3. Achievers see failures as isolated incidents.
4. Achievers keep expectations realistic.
5. Achievers focus on strengths.
6. Achievers vary approaches to achievements.

7. Achievers bounce back.

"Failure is not fatal, but failure to change may be." — John Wooden

There are times when there is no other way to fail forward than to take a risk. We have all heard the saying, "Nothing ventured, nothing gained." The following table compares the approach of two different types of people. What type of person do you want to be? (See Figure 1.)

> **"I think of mistakes as lessons that serve as fuel for the engine that drives continuous improvement."**

"When one person hesitates because he feels inferior, the other is busy making mistakes and becoming superior." — Henry C. Link

When you have the right mental attitude, failure is neither fatal nor final. What appears to be failure is usually nothing but a temporary defeat. The difference between success and failure often depends on how an individual views mistakes. If you want to continue down the road of success, Maxwell provides the following guidelines to help change the way we think about failures:

• Appreciate the value of failure — Thomas Edison appreciated the value of failure; "I have not failed. I've just found 10,000 ways that won't work."

• Don't take failure personally — No one can call you a failure but yourself. If you blame yourself or others for mistakes, there will be no improvements.

• Let failure redirect you — If you are experiencing failure and you want to fail forward, make some adjustments or try something new and different to change direction.

• Keep a sense of humor — Don't take yourself so seriously. If you can find humor in your failures, it will be easier to move forward.

• Ask why, not who — When something goes wrong, the general tendency is to look for someone or something to blame. When you play the blame game you don't take responsibility for your actions and you can't learn from the mistake. Do you remember the lesson of Event + Response = Outcome?

• Make failure a learning experience — Learning from our mistakes and failures allows us to make changes so we can improve and avoid repeating and getting what we do not want. If you keep on doing what you have always done, you will keep on getting what you have always gotten.

• Don't let failure keep you down — Sri Swami Sivananda said, "There is something good in all seeming failures. You are not to see that now. Time will reveal it. Be patient." Winston Churchill said, "Success is going from failure to failure without losing your enthusiasm."

• Use failure as a gauge for growth — Can you look back on a time in your life where a failure allowed you a new path toward success? When we take on new challenges and try new things, we grow as a person.

18

• See the big picture — Have you ever heard the phrase about getting lost in details, "Don't lose the forest for the trees"? Looking at the big picture will bring us away from putting too much emphasis on the failure or mistake we make. When I was young and messing up constantly, my grandmother would always tell me, "This too shall pass."

• Don't give up — Never, never, never give up. If you do, you are finished. "Many of life's failures are people who did not realize how close they were to success when they gave up," Thomas Edison said. The bottom line is that we are all going to fail at times in our lives. What we must each determine is whether we are going to fail backward or forward. So what do you choose?

Two magic questions exercise: Write down the answers to the next two questions. Practice a form of "mind storming" by forcing yourself to generate 20 answers to each question. The great number of ideas and improvements you come up with will astonish you.

1. What did I do right?
2. What would I do differently?

Figure 1

Don't-Dare-Try-It People

They resist opportunities.
They rationalize their responsibilities.
They rehearse impossibilities.
They rain on enthusiasm.
They review their inadequacies.
They recoil at the failure of others.
They replace goals with pleasure.
They rejoice that they have not failed.
They rest before they finish.
They resist leadership.
They remain unchanged.
They replay the problem.
They rethink their commitment.
They reverse their decision.
Motto: I would rather try nothing great and succeed than try something great and fail.

Don't-Dare-Miss-It People

They find opportunities.
They finish their responsibilities.
They feed on impossibilities.
They fan the flame of enthusiasm.
They face their inadequacies.
They figure out why others failed.
They find pleasure in the goal.
They fear futility, not failure.
They finish before they rest.
They follow leaders.
They force change.
They fish for solutions.
They fulfill their commitments.
They finalize their decisions.
Motto: I would rather try something great and fail than try nothing great and succeed.

Starting Over

(Heard)

Every day, as the sun breaks over the horizon, we begin a new life. Many of us take life for granted because, for the most part, our routines are the same.

However, I feel that entrepreneurs and business owners have a lot in common with individuals who have lost everything in natural disasters like Hurricanes Katrina, Rita and Ike because we know that every day brings new challenges and opportunities. Making the wrong decision or simply being in the wrong place at the wrong time can lead to devastating losses — including financial resources, property and even loved ones.

When it comes to starting over with a business, there are so many things that can be overlooked. There are many details to remember, of course, but starting over is easier when we remember to apply a few important principles.

First, the ability to adapt to change is a cornerstone of successfully starting over. A few years ago, I asked everyone in our company to read *Who Moved My Cheese* by Spencer Johnson and Kenneth H. Blanchard. This is a short, easy-to-read book with a very poignant message: Change can be a blessing or a curse, depending on your perspective. It's up to you to make change a positive aspect of your business — or your personal life.

It's absolutely essential to maintain a positive mindset and to think of our problems as challenges and our adversities as adventures. Most of us hate problems and adversity, but we welcome adventures and challenges that can be overcome.

Many people and businesses that are starting over have a great opportunity to do things differently — or even better. Perhaps entrepreneurs will do more market research before they begin a new business. Job seekers may choose to go in with more knowledge than before about their profession. Those who have previously shunned the latest technological advancements may now see them as a necessity. I don't think there's anyone or any company out there who can't stand to improve in some way.

In addition to a positive attitude, I believe and know from personal experiences that we must have undying faith, a willingness to work hard and perseverance.

Survival is a great motivator, whether it's trying to stay alive during or after a hurricane, trying to get a roof over our heads, finding food and water, or keeping a business going. Starting over isn't easy, but the simple fact is that when you're struggling for survival, there is no other option. You can give up and die or live in poverty and ignorance forever, or spend every waking hour learning and working.

Those who don't have jobs should spend as much time as possible learning more about their field and seeking employment. They should be willing to start at the bottom and work longer and harder than their peers. Starting over never involves a 40-hour work week — it may mean working from daylight to dark and on weekends. It means beginning as early as you can and working as long and as hard as you can until you absolutely can't go on any longer.

This same advice goes for business owners.

Starting over means keeping up your spirits while others around you are losing theirs. It means not complaining and looking for the ray of sunshine in the middle of the storm.

I've had to start over in every phase of my life — spiritual, professional and personal. When my first business failed in 1982 and I lost everything, I put myself under the microscope. I told myself that if I was going to die, I'd die working. I vowed to master every marketing technique utilized by the businesses and

" Starting over means keeping up your spirits while others around you are losing theirs."

industries we served and to develop new methods that nobody had seen. I saw starting over as a chance to do things bigger and better.

It took more than 10 years of hard work, perseverance and faith just to see the light at the end of the tunnel. Again, it wasn't easy. At one time I was almost homeless and had to depend on loved ones and friends for places to live and transportation to work. I know for a fact that people will help you if you're willing to work harder than anyone else — and that you must keep a smile on your face if you want people to care more about you. I feel this is true whether you're a business owner, a company CEO or an employee near the lower end of the totem pole.

I also believe in the old saying that "givers get" — even when they don't have a nickel in their pockets. We've got to give those who help us the confidence that we are striving for better days and that their investments will be worthwhile.

Last, but not least, don't be afraid to ask for help. People helped me because I believed in God, was willing to work hard and was courteous even in dire circumstances. This formula will work for you, too.

Take it one day at a time, find work of any kind, and strive to be the hardest and nicest worker in your environment. Out of adversity comes not only an adventure you'll always remember but also new opportunities. The keys are faith and hope, along with focus — not on the past, but on the future. I have found that starting over in my own life has instilled within me a burning desire to help others conquer adversity on the job and off.

Create Your Renewable Energy Source

(Whitelaw)

Energy is a big topic these days. It does not matter whether we are talking about the nonrenewable energy sources we use to heat our homes, run our cars or fuel our industries. Pick up a paper today and you will easily find one of the following news headlines: "Energy experts sound alarm over oil"; "Who's to blame for $4 a gallon gas?"; "Will we run out of energy?"; "How will high energy prices change day-to-day life?"

Not to disappoint you, but this article is not about that kind of energy. Now that I have your attention with this negative news, I want to talk about the energy crisis we are having with our bodies and minds.

Are you or someone you know constantly fatigued, or do you have a work group that seems like they could use an octane boost? I read a statistic that every day 2.2 million Americans complain of being tired. If this is the case, what if there were some simple things we could do to recharge our lives and improve the way we feel at work and home?

Have you been introduced to the author and speaker Jon Gordon? I read and recommend his first book, *Energy Addict: 101 Physical, Mental, and Spiritual Ways to Energize Your Life*, which focused on some practical ways to eat, sleep, breathe and exercise our ways back to higher energy and better health. His latest books are more business focused and provide us some nice simple concepts on how to remove work place negativity and increase worker productivity. Gordon and his books have been featured on CNN, NBC's Today Show and in *Forbes, Fast Company, O Magazine, The Wall Street Journal* and *The New York Times*. He has also been featured with clients such as the Jacksonville Jaguars, the PGA Tour, Campbell's, Northwestern Mutual, Publix Super Markets and JP Morgan Chase.

Understanding our energy levels

I would like to think that in some circles I might be considered knowledgeable on topics involving energy. I have been working in the energy industry for the past 25 years, I live in Houston — the energy capital of the world — and I even hold a master's degree in energy management. However, when it comes to understanding my own energy levels and learning how to turn negative energy into positive achievement, I have a beginner's mind and I am all ears. Read what Gordon says about our real energy crisis and see if this rings true to you.

"Turn the page of any paper or turn on any news show and you'll likely hear about the global energy crisis and soaring gas prices," said Gordon. "But I'm convinced that the real energy crisis is not taking place in the oil fields of Texas and Iraq, or the gas stations of New York and California but rather inside the people and the companies that contribute to our global economy.

"In a recent survey conducted by Harris Interactive Inc., less than 15 percent agree that they feel strongly energized by their work and only 20 percent feel very passionate about their jobs. While part of this crisis can be attributed to management (37 percent of managers are indifferent to their company's fate), a big part of the problem can be associated with worker burnout. Forty-two percent are coping with burnout while 33 percent believe they have reached a dead end in their jobs, and 21 percent are eager to change their jobs. The cost of fatigue, burnout and a lack of engagement to corporate America is staggering. The Gallup organization estimates the cost to be $250 billion-$300 billion, while work place fatigue alone costs American businesses at least $77 billion per year, according to the National Sleep Foundation."

" Work place fatigue alone costs American businesses at least $77 billion per year, according to the National Sleep Foundation."

In his book *Good to Great*, Jim Collins says, " ... to build a successful organization and team you must get the right people on the bus." His research shows that great companies and organizations do this. They get the right people and put them in the right seats. Collins also talks about getting the wrong people off the bus.

I think the next question is what type of fuel is required to energize the people and the bus? I think Gordon has some of the right answers to this question in his new book, *The Energy Bus: 10 Rules to Fuel Your Life, Work and Team with Positive Energy.*

The Energy Bus reveals 10 secrets for approaching life and work with the kind of positive, forward thinking that leads to true accomplishment at work and home. All of us face challenges, and to be successful every person, organization, company and team has to learn how to overcome negativity and adversity that comes our way. No one goes through life untested, and the answer to these tests is positive energy. *The Energy Bus* tells a story where people create positive energy consisting of vision, trust, optimism, enthusiasm, purpose and spirit that defines great leaders and their teams. If you are a team leader or manager looking for some help, check out the following 10 rules you can use to fuel yourself and your team.

Ten rules for the ride of your life:
1. You're the driver of the bus.
2. Desire, vision and focus move your bus in the right direction.
3. Fuel your ride with positive energy.
4. Invite people on your tour bus and share your vision for the road ahead.
5. Don't waste your energy on those who don't get on your bus.
6. Post a sign that says "No Energy Vampires Allowed" on your bus.

7. Enthusiasm attracts more passengers and energizes them during the ride.
8. Love your passengers.
9. Drive with purpose.
10. Have fun and enjoy the ride.
Now get your ticket to get on the bus!

Have You Suffered Long Enough?

(Whitelaw)

Have you heard of the Navaho Forgiveness Ritual? This tribal ritual was used when someone had a grievance, wound or painful story they wanted to share. The person seeking forgiveness would meet with tribal members to tell their story three times while everyone listened with empathy and compassion. If the person seeking forgiveness came into the circle and attempted to speak the same story a fourth time, everyone would turn their backs to the speaker. The message to the speaker was: Stop! Enough! Let it go! Go home and speak of this no more! Imagine what it would be like if our friends and family would do this for us?

Do you presently have a grievance, wound or painful story that you have expressed more than three times? If everyone stopped listening to that story

> *" Your journey to emotional freedom starts with forgiveness."*

right now, could you let it go? The Navaho Forgiveness Ritual was a healing tradition derived through the insight of wise elders over many generations, who understood that if a person is permitted to speak about their story excessively, the wounds inadvertently receive the power to take on a life of their own.

If I told you that you are not your thoughts and emotions, would you believe me? If I told you that it is your choice to hang on to your story and suffer or let go of your story and heal, would you believe me? If I told you that you are the person responsible for your current pain and suffering and not someone or something out there, would you believe me? Do you really want to hang on to your pain? It is your choice!

Your journey to emotional freedom starts with forgiveness. Why do humans think it's so hard to practice forgiveness on a consistent basis? Why do humans think that if we feel anger, hatred or resentment toward someone or something we believe has harmed or wronged us, that in some strange way we are punishing them? The longer you hold on to a painful story,

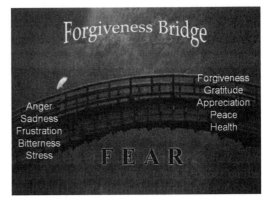

Forgiveness Bridge

Anger
Sadness
Frustration
Bitterness
Stress

FEAR

Forgiveness
Gratitude
Appreciation
Peace
Health

27

the more suffering and hurt you will bring yourself. Why would you risk harming yourself?

Medical science has proven that negative emotions have a damaging effect on our bodies. When we feel angry, frustrated, disappointed or sad, stress hormones and cholesterol are released into our bodies in damaging quantities. In addition, our heart beats faster and our blood pressure rises. Medical science has proven that such behavior — over long periods of time — causes health problems to develop. Many health professionals now conclude that even cancer and serious illnesses are a byproduct of our emotional suffering.

I found these myths associated with forgiveness on the Internet with no credit indicated but felt them worthy of reflection.

1. *To forgive, we have to forget the offending behavior.* Forgetting is not part of forgiving. With forgiveness, we let go of the past in order to reclaim the present, but we do not forget that past.

2. *To forgive is to excuse the offending behavior.* Forgiveness does not in any way excuse the inappropriate actions that created our regret. We forgive for one main reason — to be free of the negative emotions associated with that regret.

3. *When we forgive, we no longer hold the person accountable for the offending behavior.* The perpetrator should always be held responsible for the offense. We can forgive and still satisfy our need for accountability, such as asking for a divorce, suing for damages or testifying against a criminal.

4. *When we forgive, we are implying that the offender is innocent, less guilty or somehow off the hook.* Forgiveness does not imply lack of guilt. In fact, the opposite is true. An act of forgiveness may lessen the perpetrator's own suffering and regret to some degree, but only if he cares. We grant forgiveness for ourselves, not for the benefit of another.

5. *To forgive, we have to reconcile with the offender.* To reconcile with someone is to re-establish a relationship with that person. Reconciliation can be part of forgiveness, but only if we choose to make it so.

6. *We should only forgive if the other person deserves it.* We forgive others because we deserve to be free of regret and the pain it has caused us. Whether the person who hurt us deserves our forgiveness has nothing to do with our decision to grant it.

7. *We only forgive in response to a request for forgiveness.* No request from the offending party is necessary for our forgiveness. We ask ourselves to forgive the other person because we benefit most from the forgiving.

8. *If we forgive, we are being disloyal to those the offending party hurt.* This misconception is a culmination of the preceding myths, which hold that forgiveness means having to forget or excuse offending behavior, reconcile with the offender, release the offender from accountability or judge the offender deserving of forgiveness. The act of forgiving releases us from hatred and grants us freedom from the perpetrator, so it is not an act of disloyalty to the person the perpetrator injured.

9. *We forgive only on the basis of certain conditions, such as getting an apology.* Forgiveness is unconditional or it is not forgiveness. If we make our forgive-

ness conditional on what the other party does, such as apologizing or promising new behavior, we have made the perpetrator the decision maker in our process of forgiving. Ironically, this kind of thinking turns our lives over to the very person who has hurt us.

10. *Forgiveness isn't valid unless the other party accepts it.* This myth is reinforced by the common phrase, "to offer our forgiveness," as if it has to be accepted to be valid. Forgiveness is not offered, it is granted.

Forgiveness is not about giving a person a free pass or letting them off the hook for doing something egregious. Forgiveness is all about relieving the pain we are holding in our mind and body so we are free to move on with our lives. The problem we face is not out there but inside us. In other words, we have created an emotional problem that can only be resolved spiritually. Forgiveness is all about releasing our feeling of being the victim and being empowered to grow with each new experience.

I want you to think of your grievance or painful story and let yourself feel all the emotions associated therein. I want you to welcome these feelings the best you can and answer the following questions. Have I suffered long enough? How great would it be to never feel any more pain or suffering associated with this story? Would it be possible for me to let this go? When?

You have suffered way too long and it is now time for you to set yourself free from your painful story!

Finding Greater Peace Through Self-Actualization

(Heard)

As I think back over the past 67 years of my life, I believe that most of us have the same dreams.

Maslow's hierarchy of needs is often depicted as a pyramid consisting of five levels. The four lower levels are grouped together as "deficiency needs," while the top level is called "being needs."

While our deficiency needs must be met, our being needs are continually shaping our behavior. The basic concept is that the higher needs in the hierarchy only come into focus once all the needs lower down in the pyramid are satisfied. The biggest level, at the bottom of the pyramid, includes our physiological needs for survival — food to eat, water to drink, sleep and perhaps a steady job. Second

> *" The top level in the pyramid of Maslow's hierarchy of needs is doing what one is destined for."*

comes safety — protection from the elements and violence as well as a stable environment in which to live and work. The third level is a feeling of belonging and love — where we need affection, friends and a place in groups. On the fourth level is esteem — both internal and external.

Internally, we seek strength, achievement, competence, confidence, independence and self worth. Externally, esteem can mean prestige, status, recognition, attention, appreciation and even dominance in a certain field of endeavor. The top level in the pyramid of Maslow's hierarchy of needs is doing what one is destined for — reaching one's full potential by making the most of one's unique abilities. I believe that level, actualization, is when a person can devote more time, energy and financial resources to making the world a better place.

It's important to understand that as our basic needs of survival and safety are met, we gravitate toward higher needs. As those higher needs are met, most people (and groups) become kinder, friendlier and more generous. We become more receptive to constructive criticism, more oriented in a positive direction, more confident, less cynical, more tolerant and understanding and more committed to worthwhile goals.

When we reach self-actualization, people tend to be more creative, more spontaneous and better at problem solving. People at the top level tend to achieve greater peace. I've found that the combination of faith and helping others has allowed me to find greater peace.

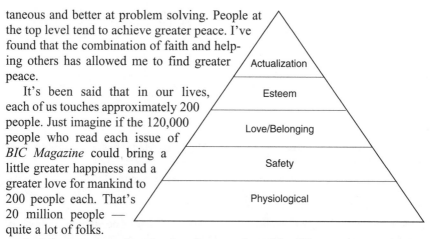

Actualization

Esteem

Love/Belonging

Safety

Physiological

It's been said that in our lives, each of us touches approximately 200 people. Just imagine if the 120,000 people who read each issue of *BIC Magazine* could bring a little greater happiness and a greater love for mankind to 200 people each. That's 20 million people — quite a lot of folks.

Let's be even more imaginative. Suppose those 20 million people could bring more love and happiness to 100 people each. That's 2 billion people. Wouldn't that be wonderful?

A few years ago, I saw on the news that television magnate Ted Turner would donate more than $1 billion over the next 10 years to causes in which he believed.

Whether or not we like Ted Turner, we cannot help but admire him for his actions. Not only is he dedicating his time and his personal resources, he is encouraging other wealthy people, in fact all of mankind, to do whatever is in their power to promote charity.

I did a great deal of soul searching in the weeks following my 1997 carjacking to determine how we at BIC Alliance could do all in our power to help others not only become more productive but also more community-conscious and family-oriented and to have a greater appreciation for life.

Even life's saddest, most challenging or most terrifying experiences can help us develop a happier, safer, more meaningful life if we can put them in perspective and gain some meaning from them.

One of the most meaningful aspects we can derive from these unpleasant experiences is keeping them in mind and passing the word along so that others are prepared when they face similar situations. Remember, from experience comes wisdom — we're less likely to get burned ourselves if we listen to and heed the words of wisdom from those who have been burned before us.

How to Successfully Plan and Execute a Personal Turnaround

(Heard)

Folks in business and industry are keenly aware of what a turnaround is and its importance. When a facility has been running at full capacity for a long time, a turnaround must be performed to make the plant run safer and more efficiently. It takes a well-trained and coordinated team of individuals numbering in the hundreds or thousands to plan and execute a successful turnaround.

In a business setting the word "turnaround" refers to wholesale changes that are made in the management or operation of a company that will lead to higher productivity and profitability. While many of us are experts in planning, managing and executing turnarounds in an industrial facility or a business setting, it takes a special set of skills to perform turnarounds in our personal lives.

One of my favorite reminders of this human flaw comes from a verse in the Bible. "Why do we so often look at the splinters in the eyes of others when we have planks in our own?" The simple truth is that many of us who are renowned as experts in things like turnarounds don't ever see the need to make repairs in our own lives.

> *" What lies behind us and ahead of us pales in comparison to what lies within us. "*

I attended a presentation given by renowned Canadian publisher, motivational speaker and author Peter Legge at the 2008 Publishing Business Conference & Expo in New York City. In his speech, Legge shared many wonderful life lessons that I was anxious to share with our *BIC Magazine* readers and BIC Alliance marketing partners. The one that immediately comes to mind relates to our tendency to let what Legge calls "un-wow" creep into our lives. Un-wow can take over when we neglect the "wow" factor in our careers and our relationships with our families, friends and business associates. I have always used the word "wow" to describe not only performance that goes above and beyond satisfactory but also the attitudes and behaviors that lead to it on a consistent basis.

Legge's discussion of wow and un-wow really hit home with me because just moments before he had the audience participate in his "Runway of Life" activity. He had each of us draw a line moving from a zero on the left side and the age of our life expectancy on the right. He then asked us to draw a star on the position along the line that best represented our present ages. In my case, I used age 84 as my life expectancy and put a star by the age I was at the time — 65. That gave me about 19 more years on the Runway of Life.

Some of our readers are much younger than I am and some are older. A lot of you probably fall within 20 years of me in either direction. No matter how old we are, however, it is never too late to turn around when we're on the Runway of Life. When I think of the many reasons why we'd want to execute a turnaround in our personal lives, the creeping in of un-wow is a good one. It stands to reason that if we find ourselves losing direction, passion or energy in our careers or in our relationships with family and friends, we should do whatever it takes to turn that around. When an industrial facility isn't operating at peak efficiency, it will be less productive or less safe — or both. When we aren't managing our lives at peak efficiency, our work and relationships will suffer in ways that can be difficult to repair if we don't take immediate action.

I've added my own twist to the Runway of Life. If you can imagine your own runway, add a star to the point at which you achieved your "inner smile." If you're not familiar with that term, I use it to refer to what we experience when we've achieved a near-perfect combination of peace, happiness and success in our professional and personal lives. For some people, the inner smile happens when they achieve fame and fortune or success on the job. Others say it occurs when we believe that there's a God or simply when we begin to make others No. 1 instead of ourselves. (A great way to make others No. 1 is to be courteous and give at least three sincere compliments to each person with whom you interact every day.) I believe the greatest wow of all comes when we bring greater peace, happiness and success to others.

Not long before I penned this column, we learned of the deaths of two very successful and well-known Gulf Coast businessmen. One was known for his love of mankind and sense of duty with regard to helping others. The other is remembered for his flamboyant lifestyle and bitter business rivalries. Which man do you think had the broadest inner smile?

I relate this story to illustrate how finite the Runway of Life really is. These two men had long and fulfilling lives, and we can only imagine how much more they would have achieved if they had lived for 20 or 30 more years. Even though we can't say for sure when we will pass on, we must not take any day of our lives for granted. In my opinion, the best way to avoid taking life for granted is to put on a smile each day, try to make your business and personal relationships as productive, peaceful and satisfying as possible, and help others who may have allowed un-wow to creep into their lives.

A great example of a person who never allowed un-wow to creep in is my father, Leo Heard, who passed away in 1996. Although he was declared legally blind at the age of 38 and was laid off from his job at a plant two months before he was eligible for disability retirement, he never complained about his lot in life. After losing his job at the plant, he began working at a hospital concession stand for the blind, where he would make his living for the next 20 years. Without his consistent support and encouragement, my wife Bodi and I probably would not have been able to overcome the many challenges we experienced during our journey as an entrepreneurial family.

Unlike a turnaround at an industrial facility or in a business setting, it doesn't take a team to make repairs in our lives, though it's always good to count on the support of our loved ones and heed the advice of our mentors and respected colleagues. As Legge said in his speech, what lies behind us and ahead of us pales in comparison to what lies within us. That's a powerful way of saying each of us has the ability to plan and execute turnarounds in our personal lives, no matter what we've been through or how dim we believe our prospects for recovery may be.

Live With Passion

(Whitelaw)

I cannot imagine a life without passion. Passion is the fuel that provides me with the energy and enthusiasm to live a fantastic, abundant and fun-filled life. I love watching and spending time with passionate people. Passionate people are so enthusiastic that it seems they have caught something that is contagious. It should not surprise me since the word enthusiasm comes from the Greek word "entheos," which means "to be filled with God." Have you ever heard someone say, "That person is on fire"?

Do you know anyone who is filled with passion? What makes these people so different from others? Why do passionate people seem to be enjoying life at full tilt and seem to be so successful at what they are doing? What is it about passionate people that seems to be attracting others to them? Have you ever been around passionate people and wondered if they were taking or drinking something that made them act in such a way? Have you ever wanted to have that same enthusiasm, energy and passion for yourself?

" *The No. 1 reason people don't get what they want is they don't know what they want.* "

Your success is guaranteed when you express your passion and enthusiasm. Doing so, you will attract:

• People who will want to play with you, work with you and support your dreams and goals.

• Higher levels of attitude and gratitude.

• Higher levels of energy.

What is your definition of a passionate life? Wonderful, fun, exciting, thrilling, purposeful, exhilarating, fired up, motivated, energized, turned on, unstoppable, focused, on point. Does your passion come from something you were born to do or from some place deep inside you? Are you currently living with passion? If not, do you want to be passionate about what you are doing?

The Passion Test

The best book and training I have come across with regard to discovering passion is *The Passion Test* by Janet and Chris Attwood. In the foreword of this book, T. Harv Eker, CEO and president of Peak Potentials Training, writes the following: "Who of us doesn't know living our passion is the key to a happy and fulfilled life? The trick for many people, though, is figuring out what your passion really is."

I've often said, "The No. 1 reason people don't get what they want is they don't know what they want." *The Passion Test* provides the simplest, clearest way to get started on knowing what you want by getting clear on who you are.

So what is "The Passion Test"? I encourage you to go out and buy the book and find out. We cannot do this test justice in this short article. But, since I can't leave you hanging, I will provide you the short version. Still, go out and buy the book!

"The Passion Test" is a tool that helps you discover the real you. To take the test, follow these instructions:

1. Make a list of at least 10 of the most important things you can think of that would give you a life of joy, passion and fulfillment. Begin each one with a verb relating to being, doing or having that completes the sentence: When my life is ideal, I am … Close your eyes and picture your ideal life. What are you doing? Who are you with? Where are you? How do you feel?

2. Let your list sit for a while. Come back to it in a few hours or the next day. When you return to your list, compare the items on the list to identify which are the most important to you. To do this prioritization, do the following:

• If you could have No. 1 or No. 2, but not both, which would you choose? Compare the two items as if you could only have one of them.

• Continue comparing the one you choose with the next number on the list until you go through the whole list, and then label the one you chose as No.1.

• Start again, compare each item that remains (don't include the ones you've already chosen), always keeping the one that's more important. When you get to the end of the list, label the choice remaining No. 2.

• Keep going through the list until you identify your most important passions.

Take your most important passions and start developing plans on how to put them into action.

Success with passion

Passion is a great tool for success, but it will take drive and commitment on your part to make it a daily discipline. The rewards of doing this are immeasurable. Living with passion will make your hours and days fly by. It will bring more joy, excitement and pleasure into you and your loved ones' lives. Passion will bring your life more meaning and will provide you the power to get all the success you desire and richly deserve.

When you clearly know your life passions, you will gain clarity, allowing you to focus more clearly on what matters most to you. You begin to make decisions and choices about where and how you are going to invest your time, energy, money and talents. This clarity will bring you all the power and energy you will ever need to live a life of passion.

The following is a fun exercise that I created to help bring more clarity into my life. I find this a quick way for me to do more of what I love to do and less of what I hate to do. I welcome your feedback on whether this tool is helpful for you.

Personal passion exercise

Take a sheet of paper and draw a vertical line down the center. On the left, list the things you love. On the right list the things you hate. When you are done, pick out one thing in the hate list and ask the following questions:

• Do I want a different outcome to this situation than what I am getting today?

• Do I take 100-percent responsibility for the way I am responding to this situation?

• What are possible solutions or actions that I could take to change the outcome that I am currently getting right now?

• Take action on at least one of your ideas to determine if it had any effect on your current outcome. If not, continue until you improve the item to something acceptable.

A Money Clip Moment

(Heard)

Each morning when I get dressed for the day, I get my wallet, my keychain and my money clip. In the wallet, I carry pictures of my family, and whenever I open it, I see the people I love and care about.

On my keychain I have a cross that was given to me by my in-laws. Whenever I pull out my keys and see the cross, it reminds me of God's love and my responsibility to share his message with others through my actions.

Last is the money clip, where I have enough small bills to cover incidental expenses. For me it makes it easier and enables me to separate large bills from small ones as a security measure.

But the main thing I enjoy about using the money clip is the story about how I began to carry it. It changed my life.

One rainy evening near dusk in the mid-1980s, I was going to try to make one last sales presentation before calling it a day. From experience, I'd learned that by starting earlier and working later I could gain access to the top decision makers because often their "gatekeepers" hadn't come to work yet or had left for the day.

> " *In order to succeed, we have to think beyond the situation we're currently in.* "

I saw a light on and a car in the parking lot at a health club owned by Guy and Ginger Bellelo and decided to make a cold call.

At this point in my life, I was publishing *BIC Magazine* four times a year and a women's magazine, *The Women's Coordinator* (*TWC*), six times a year. *BIC* was coming along fine, but *TWC* was a real disaster. I was broke at the time, and the only way I could come up with the money to print the publications was to work day and night.

Mr. Bellelo met me at the door, congratulated me on working late and asked me to join him for a cold drink. As we visited, he told me about the upcoming 25th anniversary of the health club and what a wonderful partner his wife was in making the business successful.

Then, impulsively, he reached in his pocket and pulled out a personalized money clip with a big wad of cash.

Mr. Bellelo said, "Earl, I've seen many successful women recognized on the cover of *TWC*, and I want my wife to be on the next issue. I'd like to see a story about her and our 25th anniversary. This way, we can thank our customers and

41

promote new memberships."

Folks, there was $5,000 cash in that money clip, but more importantly, Mr. Bellelo's request triggered the concept of companies sponsoring the front cover of our publication in order to share their successes.

My years of industrial management, fire and safety, and marketing training had taught me to think three-dimensionally in times of crisis and opportunity. In order to succeed, we have to think beyond the situation we're currently in. Instantly, I thought that if Mr. Bellelo would sponsor a front cover of *TWC* to recognize his partner, thank his customers and promote new business, then this concept was perfect for *BIC* as well.

At BIC Alliance, we call these pivotal moments in business "money clip moments." I'd always offered BIC Alliance members editorial space in addition to their advertisements, but I hadn't thought of having companies sponsor the cover around a trade show or important company milestone until that night.
Well, of course, the rest is history. The money clip moment spurred my first multimillion-dollar idea and taught me the importance of thinking outside-the-box in our professional and personal lives.

With the front cover sponsorships, I was able to pay for the printing of more publications. Later on, we introduced back cover and four-page insert sponsorships, which help us better serve our marketing partners.

It wasn't long before my wife Bodi and I selected a money clip for me to use as a constant reminder to start early, work late and think creatively. Every time I pick up my money clip, I remember that our lives can change overnight.

The Game of Life

(Heard)

I have always found one of life's great ironies to be that many of us seem more concerned with the performance and personal lives of professional athletes than we are with ourselves, our families, our friends and the companies with which we are associated.

We should realize that life is the most important game we will ever play. If we do so, we will work to better condition ourselves and our companies.

Since this is a story about teamwork and the game of life, let's start with our own beginnings. Please join me in some creative thinking as we imagine the world we live in as a giant stadium in which the game of life is played daily.

When we are born, our parents and other family members are our coaches, spectators, greatest fans and, of course, our cheerleaders. We as young players make many mistakes. We stumble and fall, we take timeouts, and we are often penalized for our mistakes.

> *" It is important to remember that our minds must be exercised like our bodies, and that in order to maintain a winning edge, we must consistently learn."*

As we grow older, most of us learn the rules of the game of life and evolve into responsible athletes who become role models for our future generations.

In this game of life, we must play a wide variety of positions, some at different times, some simultaneously. Sometimes we're the rookie, sometimes we're the seasoned pro. We must be experts at both offense and defense.

We may even be the owner of the franchise, the manager, the recruiter, the coach or the assistant coach, but always, regardless of the positions, either on the field or throughout the stadium, there are two roles that each of us play that are ongoing.

We are both a player and a spectator. Unfortunately, there are those of us who have become so out of shape mentally and physically that all we want to be is the complaining spectators — not willing to play the game ourselves, but finding no one who plays it well enough to suit us.

Even worse, some of us have become so complacent with our lot in life that we do not even bother going to the game, preferring merely to observe it from the comfort of our easy chair. Perhaps we have become so caught up in the beer and fast food commercials that our overindulgence has left us too exhausted to play

43

any role except that of bystander.

It is important to remember that our minds must be exercised like our bodies, and that in order to maintain a winning edge, we must consistently learn.

Part II:

Leadership

*"Don't tell people how to do things.
Tell them what to do and let them surprise
you with their results."*

— Gen. George S. Patton

Six Leadership Strategies

(White)

Some people believe leaders are born, some say they are "called," and others contend they are "made" by the times. However leaders come into being, they are in demand in the new millennium.

Contemporary leadership theorists are returning to the trait theory of leadership. They are finding that certain demonstrable qualities are shared by leaders. A number of those qualities are listed below. Determine which of these you associate with yourself:

- Do you communicate?
- Are you self-confident?
- Do you develop teams?
- Are you ethical?
- Do you share knowledge?
- Do you envision?
- Are you motivated?
- Do you follow through?
- Do you energize others?
- Do you welcome change?
- Do you do research?
- Do you help organize?

> **"It is important for leaders to communicate their values to those they lead, because those values are the foundation on which everything else is built."**

These are all essential qualities followers expect in a leader. How these expectations are met or are not met is what determines a leader's credibility factor. Credibility may well be one of the most difficult attributes for a leader to earn, as well as one of the easiest to lose.

According to Jim Kouzes and Barry Posner, authors of *The Leadership Challenge*, there are six strategies leaders can take to build and maintain their credibility. I will summarize these strategies for you to consider. I also encourage you to assess yourself in relation to how you are currently leading those for whom you are accountable.

Strategy No. 1: Clarify your values

It is important for leaders to communicate their values to those they lead, because those values are the foundation on which everything else is built. Conveying who you are, your goals and what you stand for can have a significant impact on your followers' performance and attitudes.

Strategy No. 2: Identify what your followers want

Followers are unanimous in naming responsiveness to their needs and concerns as a key factor they look for in a leader. Leaders who act only in their own self-interest, ignoring the needs of their followers, eventually lose the trust of those they lead.

Strategy No. 3: Build consensus

Followers want leaders who trust the experience and ideas of those they lead; they want leaders who seek and respect their input. While followers understand that it is the leader who must ultimately make the decision, they also know that credible leaders include and involve their followers in charting a course and setting standards. When a leader doesn't collaborate with his team, the message the team receives is that their ideas are not important or trustworthy. This is not a message that contributes to a leader's credibility.

Strategy No. 4: Communicate shared values with enthusiasm

Enthusiasm emerges as a crucial characteristic of leadership. Followers want and need leaders who can communicate shared values with ardor and conviction. They want leaders who have energy, who become involved, and who express their genuine passion for what the organization is working to accomplish. Enthusiasm is contagious. Followers catch it from their leaders. As Posner reminds us, "You can't light a fire with a wet match."

Strategy No. 5: Stand up for your beliefs

Followers don't follow leaders who lack confidence in their own decisions. While leaders must be open to alternatives and listen to feedback, they must also take a stand. Leaders who do not stand by their beliefs create stress, indecision and conflict within their team.

Strategy No. 6: Lead by example

Followers expect their leaders to do more than lead; they expect them to teach and develop leadership within their organization and to do this by setting an example. People believe actions over words every time. To be credible, a leader must be a role model. Leaders cannot hold others responsible for shared values when they don't live by those values themselves.

A final word: Leadership is not about doing it yourself. It is about building relationships with others as representatives build relationships with clients. At the heart of those relationships is credibility. A leader's credibility and believability are what enable others in any organization to achieve excellence and experience success.

Before Hiring — Defining Job Requirements

(Phillips)

The first secret to attracting and hiring the best people is to clearly understand who the best people are when it comes to your position. Not in general, but specifically for your company and for the job you have to fill.

We must accurately define the "best" person for our position in terms that will allow us to know that person when we see them.

Three ideas of the 'best' candidate

Bob Hampton, my first sales manager at Xerox, selected me to move from the "rookie team" to take my first territory. He took a lot of heat at the time, because there were several rookie candidates with more tenure on the team and traditionally promotions were handed out based on tenure and experience. Later I asked him why he broke protocol to promote me. He introduced me to his concept of "best candidate."

" Behavior defines how a person will act or react when faced with various situations. "

"Rick," he said, "In my experience, you have the three qualities of the best sales reps I've ever known. You have a powerful ego, which means you will work hard to be recognized as No. 1 — you hate to lose. Next is greed, which means you will never settle or plateau. You will continue to grow to earn the most you can because you know people recognize you by how much you sell and earn.

"Finally," he explained, "You have empathy which means you won't abuse your customers to accomplish the first two."

Bob's theory may not work for you, but someone in the organization has to define the characteristics of the best person for your job opening. I recommend looking to three sources.

The person's manager should have a clear vision of who would fit the job. The sales manager knows what needs to be done and knows what type of person has worked out well in that position before and he should also know what type of person has not worked out in the past.

The "hands on" CEO, owner or president will have thoughts on a description of "best." The person at the top is responsible for the organization's culture and future. He may be looking for an eventual replacement for the manager or a person who could eventually manage a new division.

The third person with an idea of "best" characteristics is the person in the job. Past or current salespeople have a unique vision of what is required to be successful in their position.

Once we synthesize all of the opinions, we have a much clearer vision of hiring requirements for our target "best" candidate. Now, we need some criteria to work from. There are three principle criteria to consider in the selection process — skill, knowledge and behavior. Skills are the abilities to do the job required, and are learned through on-the-job training or formal education. We need to define what is required to do the job.

Knowledge is an understanding of the job on one or many levels. It is possible to be skilled at doing a job, yet lack the knowledge that would be required to go beyond the basic activity.

Behavior defines how a person will act or react when faced with various situations. Do you need a person who is good with people or one who is focused on details? Do you need a person who can multitask or do you need someone who will not become bored when repeating the same task over and over? Studies have shown a very high correlation between behavior style and job performance in virtually every type of job.

Skills

There is a set of skills a salesperson is expected to possess. He should have probing skills to identify prospect and customer needs. He should have well-developed listening skills, negotiation skills and the skill to ask for the order. Some positions will require more telephone skills than others.

To be certain we understand the skills required another team of advisors might be necessary. This time upper-management is seldom needed for this team — they are usually too far removed from the "street." Instead, ask the sales management team and street sales people which skills are necessary and which skills should be avoided. For instance, used car selling skills may be out of place in many industries.

When lists are completed, I recommend you interview each person on the team, if even for a few minutes, to clarify the skills each has added to their list. The entire list will ultimately become a part of the job description.

Knowledge

Once we identify the skills necessary to do the job, we must uncover what knowledge the applicant needs to have for this particular job. In sales, much of the "knowledge" is product knowledge — the ability to recognize which product will fill a particular need. A key principle to recognize is that someone with all of the product knowledge in the world will not be a good salesperson without the necessary selling skills. And, frankly, the opposite is equally true. A candidate with great selling skills will be at a serious disadvantage selling welding supplies when he is working against a competitor with several years' experience. Fortunately, these inadequacies can be overcome — that's what training is all about. Once again, ask your team of advisors for a list of knowledge assets they believe a top salesperson will need in your organization.

Behavior

While "behavior" is usually the most difficult of the three criteria to accurately characterize, it may be the most valuable tool for predicting success. "Behavior" addresses how much effort a person will spend on a project, how important details and accuracy are to the candidate and even how someone treats others.

Someone once told me that, "The best predictor of future behavior is past behavior." I've found this to be true, because behavior is grounded so deeply in habits. Ask a smoker why he always lights a cigarette when starting his car. Ask a jogger why he exercises at a certain time each day. Ask a salesperson why he interrupts the prospect or why his selling day doesn't start until after 9 a.m. He will explain a litany of reasons and I'll show you a series of behaviors based on habits. This is important because once your consulting team gives you a list of behaviors of the best salespeople, you can develop interview questions that address and uncover habits that affect the desired behaviors.

If getting up early is a desired behavior, one question may be, "Sparky, tell me when you like to make your first call in the morning." Some candidates will tell you he can't make the first call until after 9 a.m. because no one is open before then. Another candidate will explain that he likes to have coffee with a prospect at 7:30 a.m. because that is when the decision maker has the fewest interruptions.

Inspire Team Success

(Whitelaw)

Michael Jordan was a great basketball player. In a team sport typically dominated by an individual member, Michael (or MJ) successfully led Chicago Bull team members to six NBA Championships by developing a great personal success plan. What was his plan, you ask? It was to inspire, to encourage other team members to a greater focus on "their" individual basketball skills and in doing so he successfully elevated the performance of everyone, including himself. Why can't we employ the same personal success plan for our workplace?

Today's complex and rapidly changing environment suggests people work in concert to solve daily business problems and challenges. If you are working in an industrial setting, it is highly probable that you are an important player on a work team. The success of a work team, like a sports team, depends on your performance as well as each team member.

How would you like to have a tool chest full of items that could help inspire you and your team? Would you be surprised to know that you already have the right tools for the job? These tools may be a little rusty and you may have misplaced some of them, but if you look around, you will find everything you need. The tools I am talking about include: attitude with gratitude, responsibility, purpose, vision, goals, passion, action, relationships, trust and contribution.

Success tool No. 1: Have an attitude of gratitude

It is critical to have a great attitude. Mix in some good old fashioned gratitude and you will set the table for success. Attitudes can be contagious, good or bad. Who would you rather work with, a person with a good attitude or one with a lousy attitude? We all have been on teams with some individuals who loved to pull down the group. What a waste of time, energy and money! Jim Collins, in his classic book, *Good to Great*, says you have to get the right people on the bus and get the wrong people off the bus. Thomas Jefferson said it very well in this quote, "Nothing can stop the man with the right mental attitude from achieving his goal; nothing on earth can help the man with the wrong mental attitude."

Success tool No. 2: Take responsibility

If you are going to inspire team success, you have to take responsibility for your role. That means you have to give up all your complaining, blaming and waiting on others to make it right. Taking responsibility is about stepping up your game and making choices that will create the results you want. Look for the behavioral signs of blaming, criticizing, complaining, condemning and cynicism to tell you if you or your team is accepting responsibility. Inspired teams discover they can't find success by making excuses.

Success tool No. 3: Discover your purpose

The team needs a clear defined purpose. Purpose is the internal compass that keeps everyone intently focused on the path of success. What does the team want to be, do or have? A clearly articulated purpose will be the foundation for building a success plan. As long as you stay on your clearly defined path, your team will stay inspired. It is important to know where you are going so you will you know when you arrive.

Success tool No. 4: Have an inspired vision

We have all learned the proverb, "Where there is not vision, the people will perish." Inspired teams need inspired visions. In my opinion, there is no more important role in life than achieving our visions while being on purpose. Make sure your vision is clear and specific. Communicate in writing what you desire to achieve and create a vision that is worthy of accomplishing and something the team will find of value. Remember the wise words of Michelangelo, "The greater danger to most of us is not that our aim is too high and we miss it, but that it is too low and we reach it."

Success tool No. 5: Create goals

Goals are the mile markers on your road to success. I like to think that a goal is a vision with a measurement and a deadline. Following are five steps to help you create inspired goals:
• Be specific on exactly what you want to accomplish.
• Write down your goals.
• Set a deadline for your goals and remember to make them SMART! (Specific, Measurable, Achievable, Realistic and Time Sensitive.)
• Chunk down all the steps and tasks required to achieve your goals.
• Organize your list into a plan.

Success tool No. 6: Live with passion

"Follow your passion, and success will follow you." — Arthur Buddhold.

Passion is an intense emotion, compelling feeling, enthusiasm or desire for anything. This passion, we speak of is your energy and it comes from bringing more of YOU into everything you do. I believe it is easier to live with passion when you love what you do and do what you love! Being passionate about a task and expressing a more genuine interest and liking for a task at hand typically uplifts people working with you. Team members will often feed off of your passion, so make sure you are contagious with passion!

Success tool No. 7: Take inspired action

Nothing happens until you take action. When you are inspired by a great purpose, everything will begin to work for you. Allow me to direct your attention to the last six letters of satisfaction, which spells "action." The dictionary defines "action" inspired as, "to cause, guide, communicate or motivate as by divine or supernatural influence." Certainly, there is always a risk element to taking action, but if you trust in yourself and "the divine," you will succeed! My thought is: when you are strongly committed to doing something and feel the urge to take action, just do it. Inspired "team action" will likely guarantee satisfaction.

Jack Canfield provides some good advice regarding this success tool. "As you begin to take action toward the fulfillment of your goals and dreams, you must realize that not every action will be perfect. Not every action will produce the desired result. Not every action will work. Making mistakes, getting it almost right, and experimenting to see what happens are all part of the process of eventually getting it right."

> *" The success of a work team, like a sports team, depends on your performance as well as each team member."*

Success tool No. 8: Create strong relationships

"The most important ingredient we put into any relationship is not what we say or what we do, but what we are." — Stephen R. Covey

Most of us are in the people business and teams are comprised of people. According to the *Ezine* article from Susan McLeod, "Six Ways to Create Strong Relationships," there are six tips to C-R-E-A-T-E stronger relationships: C is for commit. Make a decision to commit yourself fully to your team. R is for recognize. See every person on your team for who they truly are and be grateful for the talents, strengths and gifts they contribute. E is for engage. Be enthusiastic, available and involved with your team and their efforts. A is for accept. Everyone is different and unique and should be accepted as equals among the team. T is for trust. Get out of the way and trust that your team will deliver the results you desire. E is for energize. Keep the energy high by taking the pressure off the team and making things fun.

Success tool No. 9: Build trust

Dr. Covey wrote a wonderful book, *The Speed of Trust*. Covey builds the case that "trust" is the one notion that changes everything and nothing is as fast as the speed of trust. To inspire a team, it is critical to establish, grow, extend, and (where needed) restore trust among team members. Covey introduces 13 behaviors that we can use to be a high-trust leader. These behaviors are as follows:

1. Talk straight
2. Demonstrate respect
3. Create transparency
4. Right wrongs
5. Show loyalty
6. Deliver results
7. Get better

8. Confront reality
9. Clarify expectation
10. Practice accountability
11. Listen first
12. Keep commitments
13. Extend trust

The best leaders recognize that trust impacts us 24/7, 365 days a year. Building trust is essential to achieving success, for it impacts the quality of your relationships, communication, work projects, team ventures and ultimately your desired results.

"Our distrust is very expensive." — Ralph Waldo Emerson

Success tool No. 10: Make a contribution

"Always render more and better service than is expected of you, no matter what your task may be." — Og Mandino

Everyone on an inspired team wants to be a contributor and provide valuable service. The more you give to the team, the more the team will give back. When your focus changes from self to others, your sense of joy, contentment and self-worth greatly soars.

You now have a "chest of success tools" available for your use. Take action today to utilize them for team and/or personal tasks — to achieve fantastic results.

"Coming together is a beginning. Keeping together is progress. Working together is success." — Henry Ford

The Traits of an Effective Leader

(Heard)

In preparing for this piece, I went into my library of past issues of *BIC Magazine* and other literature on management and training I've gathered over the past 30 years. On the desk before me sat at least five manuals, 50 articles and a copy of Webster's New World Dictionary. Behind me were a telephone, a computer and a bookshelf with 24 books and at least a dozen magazines. Within five steps of my desk was another bookshelf with about 100 books and other pieces of resource material.

As you can tell, I've done extensive research into leadership not only to enhance my skills as a manager but also to help educate others on what it takes to be an effective leader.

It is true that leaders are made, not born. As a matter of fact, they are almost always works-in-progress. No matter how great a leader one man or woman is, he or she can always improve. And leaders are not gods, even though some may think they are. Personally, I feel that although leaders are not gods, they should follow godly principles.

> *" No matter how great a leader one man or woman is, he or she can always improve. "*

Before we discuss the making of a leader, let's examine what defines a manager. "Management" is defined in Webster's dictionary as "the act, art or manner of managing," or "handling, controlling or directing." A "manager" is "a person who manages a business, institution or family — skillfully and carefully."

A leader is defined as "a person or thing that leads; directing, commanding or guiding head, as of a group or activity." Further research defines "lead" as "to show the way or to direct the course of by going before or along with."

When we look closely at the definitions of "manager" and "leader," one glaring difference becomes evident. All leaders aren't managers, but it seems that all managers are in charge of leading somebody or something. For the purposes of this article, let's define our topic more closely by examining what it takes to make a leading manager.

I learned during my days as a management trainer that the job of management involves the ability to plan, organize, control and coordinate the use of resources to assure that they are used effectively and efficiently to reach desired goals.

Looking back over the course of my career, I can think of hundreds of great leaders who never wanted to become managers. The best that come to mind are

59

Arthur Williams, who was a mason tender, and Leon Sims, who once worked as a process operator for Ethyl Corp. Both Arthur and Leon were the best at what they did, and were recognized as leaders by their peers and managers. Although neither was a manager, both men were "go-to" guys when it came to work ethic, job knowledge and character. Most of all, they were role models not only for the craftsmen but also to those who aspired to become managers.

Another distinguishing characteristic shown by both men was the ability to lead during times of crisis. While working as a bricklayer, I was electrocuted by a brick saw. Arthur grabbed a 2x4 and used it to shove me out of harm's way. During emergency situations at the Ethyl plant, it was Leon — rather than our foremen — who showed the greatest leadership by demonstrating how to restore safety and order in a calm and systematic way.

Not long after I became a supervisor at the plant, an incident occurred in which a cylinder head blew off of a propane compressor in the middle of the night, creating a potentially disastrous and life-threatening situation. By the time I could get the sprinkler system on and a curtain of water going into the area, two of the most unlikely fellows on the shift had isolated the equipment and secured the area. I never forgot that incident because one of my fellow supervisors — a man whom I had thought was a natural leader — reacted to the situation by running off into the night like a frightened child.

Real leaders appreciate the importance of training. If a person wants to be a real leader, he needs to know what to do and how to do it. He must also know where to go for help when it is needed. Real leaders are good role models, and they know how to keep cool in times of crisis. Whether you're a CEO or a trainee, it's critical that you know who the best leaders in your company are. Often times these individuals make good trainers because people tend to learn more from those they admire and respect.

Maintaining Strong Mentor-Protégé Relationships

(Heard)

A strong management team is crucial to success in any business. They must believe in the benefits of training, and they must be involved in those training efforts. They must also know that those new employees involved in the training program need to have a full understanding of every aspect of the business, and how every department and every function of the organization interrelates. Only when they realize how each member contributes to the team will they truly be one of its members.

As team leaders, we must do our part to make certain that everyone on our team is at the top of his game. We can accomplish this by sharing our own experiences so that they learn from the games we have played in the past. The same is true of leading by example. If we settle for mediocrity in an organization, that will never be a "championship" organization.

" There are many folks who have forgotten that they started out as just another minnow in a very big pond, struggling day to day to succeed."

I sincerely believe that our leaders of tomorrow (our children, grandchildren and protégés) are anxious and excited to learn and use the knowledge they gain in their daily lives. I also feel that those of us who have accumulated that experience and knowledge should be just as excited to pass it on.

Our BIC Alliance team members who have been with us the longest seem to enjoy the mentor-protégé relationship. They take it upon themselves to help raise the level of everyone in our organization. They are quite often the ones who step forward and suggest ways we can serve our alliance members more efficiently and more effectively.

If your organization is lucky enough to include such individuals, it is your responsibility to encourage them and help them to grow every step of the way. Your business depends on it!

When Moby Dick was a minnow

There are many people who, when they reach a certain level in their careers, are so consumed with self-importance that they forget they reached that position by climbing the stairway to success one step at a time, not by suddenly appearing

61

there as if by magic.

This scenario is perfectly summed up by a comment I once heard my good friend and longtime business associate Bud Howard of Volvo make when referring to a mutual acquaintance. Bud said, "I've known him since Moby Dick was a minnow."

Unfortunately, there are many folks with whom we come in contact that, while they may now have a whale of a title, have somehow forgotten that they started out as just another minnow in a very big pond, struggling day to day to succeed. These are the folks who are too busy to return phone calls because their time is much more valuable than anyone else's. They are the ones who constantly scan the crowded room or look over the shoulder of whomever they're speaking with to see if there is someone else present who is more important.

One of my greatest pleasures in being a Moby Dick in industrial marketing is always being able to recall my days as a minnow, and the favorable impression I had of those in higher places who treated not only me but also each of us minnows as the most important person they knew.

These are the people who encourage others, the ones who make that climb up those stairs a bit easier. It is these people who should be recognized for the role they play in helping us grow from minnows to leviathans.

Be a Person of Integrity

(Whitelaw)

Every day, stories in newspapers, magazines and television reveal tales of athletes, leaders, politicians and celebrities who demonstrate a lack of integrity. Think a moment — when was the last time you heard a story about a high-profile athlete being arrested, a CEO stealing millions of dollars from the company or a well-respected politician getting caught (so to speak) with his hand in the cookie jar? Was it today, yesterday or several days ago? Regardless of when it was, I dare say you would agree that it happens much too often. Time and again, it seems as though our world is run by supposedly respectable people who are characteristically devoid of the important value known as integrity.

Reaching a higher level of success depends on an individual's ability to be a person of integrity. So what is integrity, why is it important, and how do we become a person of integrity?

I like the following definition written by Stephen R. Covey: "Integrity means we are committed to matching words, feelings, thoughts and actions, with no desires other than the good of others, without malice or desire to deceive, take advantage, manipulate or control; constantly reviewing your intent as you strive for congruence."

> **" People who possess integrity live and act in harmony with their values and beliefs."**

Integrity is the alignment and the correspondence between what we think (beliefs and values), what we say to others and what we do.

In other words, we become authentic to our true self when what we are thinking, saying and doing is one and the same.

People who possess integrity live and act in harmony with their values and beliefs. They not only talk the talk, but they walk the talk. Whenever these people feel compelled to do something, they act. Instead of being driven by the "good" opinion of others, they simply respond to the quiet voice residing within their consciousness. Do you know anyone like this?

John Maxwell, in his book, *Becoming a Person of Influence*, explains that integrity is an inside job. He says that integrity must be developed from within us. He tells us that there are three trusts about integrity that go against common thinking:

1. Integrity is not determined by circumstances. We are responsible for our choices. Our circumstances are as responsible for our character as a mirror is for

Commit Yourself to Honesty, Reliability and Confidentiality	• Make choices today to live by a strict code of conduct.
Decide Ahead of Time You Don't Have a Price	• Make a decision today that there is not enough money, power, fame or pride in the world to buy our integrity.
Major in the Minor Things	• Realize that the little things will either make or break us. We build our integrity one step at a time, over a long period of time.
Each Day, Do What You Should Do Before What You Want to Do	• Each day we should do at least two things that we have been putting off. We should complete these tasks before we do anything on our to-do list that we enjoy.

our looks. What we see only reflects what we are.

2. Integrity is not based on credentials. No number of tiles, degrees, offices, designations, awards, licenses or other credentials can substitute for basic, honest integrity when it comes to the power of influencing others.

3. Integrity is not to be confused with reputation. Worry less about what others think, and give your attention to your inner character. A friend of mine is fond of saying, "Energy flows where attention goes."

So why is integrity important? One word: Trust. Without trust, we have nothing. I believe that trust is the single most important factor in personal and professional relationships. The more trustworthy we become, the more trustworthiness we will inspire in others.

Stephen M.R. Covey's book, *The Speed of Trust*, provides us with three high-leveraged ideas that can help us to be a person of integrity:

1. Make and keep commitments to yourself. There is nothing more important than learning how to make and keep commitments, especially to ourselves. If we break a promise to ourselves, we will break promises to others. This is the key to building self-trust. I love the saying, "Make a promise — keep a promise."

2. Stand for something. If we are going to be a person of integrity, then we must know our values and what they stand for.

3. Be open. Openness is very important to integrity. If we are open, then we will be receptive to new ideas, possibilities and growth. Being open also develops

a level of trust with others and can impact both our current and future performance. When we constantly dismiss ideas, we doom ourselves to a life of status quo. Life is so much better when we are open and comfortable knowing who we truly are.

So how do we become a person of integrity? The best way I know is to practice "integrity fundamentals." Maxwell gives us the following to work on:

Integrity is an inside job. It is not easy to be a person of integrity, but the rewards are great personally and professionally when we are. When we make promises and keep promises, especially to ourselves, we build character and trust. When we commit to living a life of what we think, say and do, we will be a person of integrity.

How to Fail

(Strickland)

You were probably expecting the headline of this article to say, "How to Succeed" rather than to say "How to Fail," but often failure teaches success. Thomas A. Edison once remarked, "Results! Why, man I have gotten a lot of results. I know several thousand things that won't work."

One of the traits that I believe can contribute to failure is to be a "people pleaser." Trying to please everyone is simply impossible. I've seen this trait in many salespersons, and there are often customers/potential customers who like to take advantage of the people-pleasing sales representative. Those who think that they will be successful sales-wise just by pleasing customers can be sadly mistaken. They end up wasting a lot of time on the wrong people and investing too little in the right people. You also set your own core principles aside in your effort to get along, which makes you vulnerable in many different ways.

" By trying to specialize in everything, you specialize in nothing."

People pleasing can also apply to companies. It is important to differentiate your company from the competition and not try to be all things to all people. By trying to specialize in everything, you specialize in nothing. Would you rely upon a handyman to make major foundation repairs to your house, or would you call a foundation repair specialist?

While egomania can be an obsessive psychological abnormality, someone with just a little too much ego can be destructive also. When one's own ego grows to watermelon size, it can eat up many a good person and destroy families, businesses and friendships. I perform charity work and have noticed that those who have given in to the allure of their own ego, selfishness and self-centeredness often end up in a state of disappointment and even despair.

Extra large egos are common in politicians, but when even a politician's ego gets out of control, people notice, and voters, frankly, don't like it. Businessmen with large egos who think they know everything and refuse to take the advice of those around them can be mistaken too. Don't just automatically discard opposing viewpoints — the other guy may have a point or spark an idea. Feedback is a good thing, and a good leader is open to constructive, honest, educated and experienced feedback.

We've all experienced the chronic "excuse maker." Kids are the best at it — "It wasn't my fault; he hit me first." You've heard that. But you've also heard co-workers make excuses. Excessive excuse making can be detrimental to one's career.

President Harry Truman recognized that passing the buck or responsibility on to someone else was a bad trait in a leader, so he put a sign on his desk that said, "The Buck Stops Here." But I also like what the famed inventor, George Washington Carver said, "Ninety-nine percent of the failures come from people who have the habit of making excuses."

Now that I've listed some traits that I think contribute to almost certain failure, I'd like to turn the negative into a positive. It's almost a given that to be successful you will first experience failure in some form. But failure has a purpose if we recognize exactly why we failed and proceed to learn from that. It's called "failing intelligently." Failing intelligently means that you pack up as many lessons as possible and take them with you when you get back on track and climb that road to success.

So, be aware of your personal characteristics. You know deep down inside if you are a people pleaser, if your ego is out of control or if you are a chronic excuse maker. Of course you must first want to change and understand how that change will benefit you, those around you and your career as well.

Surviving in Business During Challenging Times

(Heard)

Following is an article that originally ran in the Summer 1985 issue of BIC *Magazine's predecessor, the* Business and Industry Coordinator. *Twenty-five years later, I still stand by those words. Today, with more than 40 years' experience in business and industry, I am proud to continue to share what I've learned with our readers.*

What is interesting to note is that on the cover of this issue was Sonny Anderson, founder of ANCO. Mr. Sonny was not just a cover sponsor of our publication, he was also one of the people that helped our company get started in the first place:

Since ancient times, man's strongest instinct is that of survival. Whether it is the prehistoric man picking up a club to protect himself against wild animals or a modern day traveler dodging a reckless driver, we all have the same natural instinct of protecting ourselves in times of danger. Everyone wants to survive!

" The greatest asset in any company is the people who make up the organization."

There are many types of survival that face today's men and women. We all have to face the challenges of physical, financial and emotional survival, but for many of us in the business community, our strongest challenge is the survival of our company.

Just as the wild animals and natural disasters threatened our forefathers, the economic conditions in our country have forced the modern day executives to resort to business survival tactics in order to prevent the death of their companies. With only one new business out of 10 lasting three years — and corporate bankruptcies at an all-time high — it is essential that every company have a business survival strategy.

Having experienced the death of a company and participated in the development of survival strategy for others, I am familiar with the techniques that are essential for business survival today.

The first and foremost ingredient that is essential to business survival is to know how your company stands at all times. Imagine going to a sporting event where no one kept score; companies are the same way. You've got to know the score at all times.

This means that you must know your financial, operational and marketing

69

status. If the departments are run by different individuals, it is essential that communications be excellent between all departments. Communication plays a key role in business survival.

If your company is in trouble, the first thing you must do is thoroughly evaluate your organization and then establish a formal plan of action. An in-depth needs analysis will pinpoint your primary challenges and will give you some ideas for solutions.

Once you have analyzed the status of your company, the next step is to develop a plan that enables your company to not only survive, but to become stronger. This is often called a business prospectus and is essential when trying to secure loans for your company.

Another key factor in business survival is to know who your key people are and how to get maximum productivity from your personnel. Performance appraisals will not only help you evaluate your personnel, but will give your poor performers the information they need to improve. How can your employees know how to do a better job unless they are properly evaluated and given the necessary feedback?

The greatest asset in any company is the people who make up the organization. You will stand or fall by these people, so they must be trained to produce maximum results at minimum expense.

When your supervisors are properly developed, they can achieve more for your company. They must be good communicators and know how to manage their time properly.

Having a strong organizational structure with job descriptions will enable your company to consolidate jobs without disruption in the organization. It is far better for some jobs to be consolidated and to lose only a few employees than to fail to take corrective action and to lose an entire company.

Employee motivation and training are essential if your company is to survive. When your employees are properly informed and treated with respect, you will have a high level of productivity and minimum turnover. This means that supervisors must know how to be supervisors and that employees should know their jobs thoroughly.

I have developed a program called the Anchor Learning Technique, which centers around the development of a cadre of key management and staff personnel who master the techniques of communication and understanding people. They then know how to help others learn their present jobs faster and more thoroughly.

Employees are also taught the same techniques, which enable them to be better communicators who understand this supervision and their fellow employees. They are first taught how to learn and then how to learn their job in a sequential manner. Training time has been cut by as much as 30 percent through the use of this technique.

(Editor's note: Many of the techniques of Anchor Learning have been interpreted in the Alligator Management & Marketing seminars presently conducted by Earl Heard.)

Your Fairy Godmother Ain't Coming

(Phillips)

"Let's see how this works," said the consultant, "in the past five years your marketplace has been in complete gyration, undergoing unprecedented transformation. Your customers have dramatically changed, the way they buy has completely changed, half of the people you are calling on are new, they are asking for more, they are much more sophisticated, negotiating harder, demanding more of your people's time, expecting to pay less and taking longer to send what they do pay. Additionally the number of businesses you sell to has changed. There are more competitors out there than ever before, offering more services than the marketplace ever dreamed of five years ago, and they are doing it faster, cheaper and more reliably than possible five years ago. Your salespeople have more confusion than focus, they are selling more and making less than five years ago and you can't reach anybody because everybody has voice mail. And you expect your business to survive and grow, managing and selling the same way you have for the past 10 years when everything else in the marketplace is unique and different?"

" If you are looking for a one-way ticket to mediocrity, just keep doing what you have always done."

Tough questions, but then few of the really important questions are easy. The problem is we have to face the really tough questions since so few of us live in a fairy tale world where all of the stories end with "they lived happily ever after." When Cinderella dreamed of going to the big dance she was fortunate enough to have the able assistance of her fairy godmother. With one wave of the wand, Cinderella was transformed from a social waif to the belle of the ball, destined to steal the heart of the handsome prince.

The bad news is, there are some businesses out there today that will never get to the ball unless they too have access to a fairy godmother. Someone needs to tell them, "Your fairy godmother ain't coming."

Change
"We have always trained our salespeople this way."

If you are looking for a one-way ticket to mediocrity, just keep doing what you have always done. If IBM, Ford and Xerox can't survive doing it the same old way, what makes you think that you can? Things are changing and what made an organization successful yesterday may not hold true today and will probably fail tomorrow.

Habits within any organization tend to perpetuate themselves, because at one time they worked. Railroads used to work well too, but they have been replaced,

71

first by the interstate system and then by cheap airfares.

You and I can't afford to hold on to "the same old way," especially if it's not working. Our sales professionals, indeed all of our employees, depend upon our leadership. They expect us to have a firm grip on what is going on in the organization, its future and the industry. Their faith in our direction and us begins to wane when they see our thinking and decision making turning habitual, predictable, inward and out of touch with reality.

Tough questions

What new skills training are you providing your salespeople? Is it making a difference? How do you know? What new information do you have on coaching your sales professionals? How much time are you spending in the field with your salespeople? What are you doing to reinforce sales training on a weekly basis? What percentage of your gross profit margin are you spending on training your salespeople? How are you managing your sales professionals differently from five years ago?

Communications

"I don't have time to talk to my salespeople."

Faced with the growing demands on leadership in most organizations, many managers have found themselves increasingly isolated from the front lines. In addition to the obvious problem of lack of accurate information, this communication vacuum has other serious side effects. The sales team may begin to feel that their input is unwanted or thought irrelevant. Worse yet, they may feel that management is avoiding the truth or intentionally creating artificial barriers from the obvious since they don't have the answers.

In his book *The Fifth Discipline*, Peter Senge says, "The hallmark of a great organization is how quickly bad news travels upward." The first tough question is how fast is the bad news reaching your desk?

How often do you set aside one hour to privately speak to each of your salespeople? How "open" is your open door policy? (If no one is using it then it's not working.) How much time are you spending traveling with your salespeople in the field, in front of customers? When was the last time you were able to ask a salesperson about one of his family members by name? How well are your salespeople communicating with their accounts ... and how do you know? When was the last time you went to a salesperson's office to congratulate the rep for an order? How often do you hold meetings outside of the office? How often do you sponsor social gatherings? How often do you review accounts one-on-one with each salesperson?

Welcome mistakes

Making mistakes means that someone is trying something. Naturally, too many mistakes can create problems, but I will submit that problems that are more serious exist if your salespeople aren't occasionally taking risks to make things happen for the organization and the customer.

Rosabeth Moss Kanter says, "Wise executives worry more about invisible mistakes — failing to take risks, failing to innovate to create new value for customers." Fear of making a mistake erects an artificial barrier that stifles creativity, innovation and growth. Mistakes can be learning experiences and the tolerance of those mistakes of enthusiasm and creativity will encourage more learning experiences and ultimately corporate progress.

What's new? When was the last time you "publicly" congratulated someone for sticking their neck out and taking a chance? How are you encouraging risk taking?

Change, communications and mistakes are just realities we must address as our organizations face the increasing demands on business today. One thing remains certain — it is up to us because we know the fairy godmother ain't coming.

Creating, Maintaining Success Through Training, Planning

(Heard)

Training is one of my greatest passions, along with helping people find greater peace, happiness and success on the job and off. Many managers and supervisors in business and industry are moving toward retirement and will soon be replaced by younger folks with little or no supervision experience who will be empowered to supervise tens of thousands of workers with little or no industry experience. This is why training is more important now than ever. There are several steps we as managers and trainers must take into consideration in order to help our employees maximize their success and personal development.

I'd like to begin by reminding everyone of the words of our good friend Shirley White of Success Images. Dr. White reminds us that we never get a second chance to make a first impression. Whether it's our first day in supervision or we've been doing it for decades, we as leaders need to have super vision in how we manage and communicate with others. This means first and foremost that we must be able to envision ourselves as the other person and treat him the same way we would like to be treated. People never forget it when we hurt their feelings or put them down — especially if we do it in front of others.

" The first and foremost step in planning is to analyze our present position by asking 'Where are we now?' "

On pages 35-37 of my book, *It's What We Do Together That Counts*, I share a story about a life changing experience I had in my early days as a supervisor at Ethyl Corp. In short, I made the mistake of treating others the way they often treated me instead of treating them the way I would like to be treated. Thankfully, my managers taught me to lead with empathy, compassion and understanding. I learned that if we are to become successful leaders we must be able to listen more, communicate better and remember that there are always two sides to every story.

Quentin Hall, who was my supervisor at Ethyl and one of my most important mentors, told me that it's not just a matter of getting something done but also getting it done diplomatically. We must always remember that there is not a big "I" or a little "u" in the word "team." It is absolutely essential for us to remember that the word "team" means "Together Everyone Accomplishes More."

We should also keep in mind that, like a chain, we're only as strong as our weakest link. We must constantly strive to improve our people skills and to learn and do our jobs better, faster and with greater cooperation. We can't, however,

75

get so busy doing our jobs that we don't take the time to train and treat others with kindness and empathy.

Matthew 7:12 — or, as it is commonly known, the Golden Rule — says "Do to others what you would have them do to you." Perhaps it is called the Golden Rule because in order for us to enjoy a golden life or earn more gold as a sales executive or manager, we must master this age-old message.

I believe that it is easy for us to establish a workplace in which everyone truly enjoys coming to work and has greater peace, happiness and success on the job and off. All we have to do as managers is lead by example and remember the "People Secret," as taught by author and sales training expert Les Giblin many years ago — when we make others No. 1, they will respond in kind.

Invest time and resources in planning

In his book *100 Ways To Bring Out Your Best*, Roger Fritz rates thinking ahead as the most important aspect of planning. Fritz goes on to say that planning is the process by which we continuously create our own future. I use what I call the five Ps — Proper Planning Prevents Poor Performance — to constantly remind others and myself about the importance of planning in our business and personal lives.

Many of us will jump into a project instead of planning out the process from A to Z. We tend to put off planning because it takes time and thought and often requires digging for information. In our Alligator Marketing & Management guide, there is an excellent diagram about how to plan by asking four questions:

1. What are we trying to accomplish?
2. How are we going to accomplish it?
3. How will we organize our resources?
4. What are our operating rules or boundaries?

After these questions are answered, I recommend reviewing the plan often and changing it as needed. The first and foremost step in planning, however, is to analyze our present position by asking "Where are we now?"

We must plan for everything that could happen, and planning must take place by everyone every day. Many companies have a tendency to invest more time in planning for now instead of also planning for the future. We also plan more on what to do in a crisis or emergency and don't devote enough time to planning on what to do if things go better than expected.

In sales, we sometimes find ourselves investing a lot more time and energy into bringing in new business than keeping the business we have. We should never forget, however, that it is four times as easy to keep existing business as it is get new business.

Of course, proper planning cannot be done without effective training. Success creates an even greater need for good training at all levels. When we hire or promote someone, we should never let that person learn on his own through trial and error. Instead, we should expect our managers to develop and implement a training game plan that will speed the learning process.

Keeping Our Minds Free of Clutter

(Heard)

In the business world and in our personal lives, we are constantly reminded of how things can go wrong due to a lack of planning. At BIC Alliance, we begin our planning for each new year several months in advance — our folks submit to me their goals for the upcoming year and accomplishments from the previous year well before the holiday season.

Proper planning requires focus and clarity because, in many cases, circumstances beyond our control force us to change course. To use a football analogy, if a head coach builds his entire game plan around a single player — a running back or a quarterback, for instance — the success of the team will depend greatly upon that player's health and effectiveness. If that player is injured or does not perform well against the opposing team's defense, the coach must make adjustments. In order to do so, he must collaborate with his players and offensive assistants to come up with a contingency plan that everyone believes will lead to

" Think of your brain as a vault in which you store your greatest treasure — knowledge."

victory. All of this must be done while the game is being played — not an easy task for the head coach since he is responsible for overseeing every aspect of his team's effort.

The key to remaining clear and focused in a relatively chaotic situation — whether it's a football game or a particularly busy work period — is to keep our minds free of clutter. Our offices and homes can become littered with trash or other displaced objects if we don't stay organized or pick up after ourselves. The same is true for our minds. Think of your brain as a vault in which you store your greatest treasure — knowledge. We all know that knowledge, when used properly, can be turned into gold in the form of opportunities both on the job and off.

Because we are not perfect, however, we often allow our minds to become littered with counterproductive and harmful thoughts and information. This input turns the mind into a garbage dump instead of a bank of opportunity.

Ask yourself this question — what thoughts fill your mind the most? Do you spend more time thinking about positive things such as opportunities for enhancing your faith, career or personal time or about the things that can prevent you from doing so? Are you focused on healthy habits or are you paralyzed by an addictive behavior or thought process?

The old saying, "garbage in, garbage out" is very applicable to our minds. If we constantly feed ourselves negative information or focus on the things we fear or believe we can't control, it will be reflected in our words, actions and achievements (or lack thereof). After all, if a football coach pays more attention to taunting from the crowd or the complaints of disgruntled players, he will not be able to turn a negative situation into a winning effort.

It is a simple truth that we become what we think about the most. It follows that if we consume positive information, whether from books, magazines, TV programs or movies, we will become more positive in our attitudes toward life's challenges and opportunities. I know from personal experience that the more we focus on positive thoughts and actions, the more quickly our lives can change for the better. We make better decisions and are able to game plan for challenges, opportunities and unforeseen events that can hamper our efforts if we're not prepared to think on our feet. We can't always control how thoughts enter our minds, but we can control how long they stay there.

Making Learning a Lifetime Experience

(Heard)

Over the past 67 years, I've found that people who help others find success are among the happiest folks I've ever met. There is just something about being around someone who is excited about what they're doing that tends to rub off on us.

In *It's What We Do Together That Counts*, I wrote a lot about the role mentors and trainers have played not only in my success but also in the success of thousands of people I've met over the years. One thing that almost every trainer I've met agrees upon is that the more they're involved in training others, the better they become at their trade or profession. Another thing that stands out about training is that those who need it most are usually the ones who seek training the least.

" There are basically two ways to learn — through our own experiences and through the experiences of others."

For example, let's think about safety and environmental training. Usually, it's the same businesses and industrial facilities that seem to have the most incidents — fires, explosions, accidents, etc. Even worse, it seems that it's the same people who keep getting hurt.

This is also true when it comes to management and sales training. It seems that it's usually the same people who are constantly making mistakes, having people problems, missing sales quotas, losing their jobs, etc.

Early in my career I learned that there are basically two ways to learn. We can learn through our own experiences, and we can learn through the experiences of others. Of course, there is nothing that hits home more than a personal experience, but it sure can help — and is a lot less painful — to learn from others.

If someone we know shows us his face and arms, seriously burned from an accident at home or work, it should help us remember not to make the same mistakes.

The same is true for management and sales. If someone can show us how to communicate more clearly, negotiate more effectively, make better presentations, manage our time more wisely or close larger accounts, it seems like we'd be foolish not to listen, learn and practice.

A few years ago, John Lake and Nick Ferris of Rain for Rent came to visit our headquarters in Baton Rouge. During our meeting, we discussed a wide range of topics including product launches, marketing strategy, recruiting and the importance of ongoing training not only in management and sales but also throughout an organization. John had some great comments in my first book about the role of CEOs and how great corporate cultures improve the character of every team member.

Personally I believe, like John, that the motivation for ongoing career training must begin with top management. When folks throughout the company see that the top executives believe in and practice ongoing training themselves, it sends a strong message to everyone.

Not only do I love to read and learn from others, I also love sharing what I've learned with family, friends and co-workers to help them become more success-ful. That's a key reason why we wrote *It's What We Do Together That Counts*, *Energy Entrepreneurs* and *Industry Achievers*.

On a more personal note, the issue of training goes back to the old question of "What's in it for me?" In life-and-death related training, we tend to be more interested in training because we know what we're learning may actually save a life or the life of a loved one or colleague. We also know that if our plant or our company shuts down, we may be out of a job — so we have a vested interest in learning all we can.

In management and sales training, the results are rarely if ever instantaneous, so the need for urgency in learning isn't life-threatening. Training our mind is like exercising our body. We don't get stronger or healthier or lose weight overnight, but with regular "training," we can make phenomenal improvements.

Now, let's take a look at the issue of "What's in it for me?" beginning with top management. The simple fact is that the better trained your management and sales force is, the more successful your company is. In addition, you'll have fewer people problems, less turnover, better customer relations and higher renewals of business. Ultimately, the proper training of your personnel results in more time for you to enjoy life and experience greater peace. The advantages are the same not only for your management and sales force but also throughout the company.

As I've said before, the journey to success begins with taking that first step. Why not make that first step a commitment to making training a positive, ongo-ing lifetime experience? After all, today is the first day in the rest of our lives.

Rested and Ready

(Brinsko)

As a leader, odds are you spend 45-60 hours (maybe more) per week on the job. It is no secret that Americans work longer days and weeks with shorter vacations than workers in any other nation. I've always found that mid-year is a good time to take a break, get some rest, review goals and prepare mentally for the second half of the year.

At BIC Alliance, we have a running joke: we only work half days and we also have flex time — you can choose to work any 12 hours a day you want! Seriously though, I am amazed at the steadfast determination and dedication of our production staff; each month they work additional time in the middle of our press period, cramming in an extraordinary amount of productivity into a workday. They accomplish all this, plus they work on a new Web site and take initiative to freshen the look of our flagship, *BIC Magazine*. Wow.

" No success at the job makes up for a failure at home."

We like to joke, but we have a serious creed as well: no success at the job makes up for a failure at home. Success at home usually involves some kind of break from the job; it means not focusing on career, at least for the moment. With a spouse, it might be a chance to reconnect. With your kids, you might create or deepen bonds. With your family, you will experience life and create memories. With yourself, it might be only a necessary recharge for your batteries, or it might go as far as helping you keep your sanity. I believe that we are created with taking breaks in mind; that is, we are programmed to perform better when we periodically rest.

This is absolutely necessary to prevent burnout and to give much needed time to your family and to worship as you choose. If you believe in God, it is appropriate to note that taking that day off isn't just recommended, it is commanded — "Six days you shall labor, and do all your work, but on the seventh ... you shall not do any work."

When folks think of a break, we naturally think of a vacation. However, taking a break might mean just having a little quiet time during the day. I like to get up early and have quiet time in the house. During this time, I can plan my day, think about life, study scripture and pray. I know it allows me a chance to be more productive overall, even though I may not be "accomplishing" much during this break time.

Most of our staff takes vacation during the summer months; it is one of the

81

reasons a single issue of *BIC Magazine* covers both June and July. At the time of this writing, I had recently returned from taking a family vacation. I hadn't felt more relaxed or rested since the last time I took a big break. I would encourage anyone to take the time to rest, reconnect with your family and recharge for work, no matter the size or significance of your responsibilities on the job.

Part III:

Professional Development

"Success is the sum of small efforts, repeated day in and day out."

— Robert Collier

Body Talk: Communication or Confusion

(White)

"Actions speak louder than words." How often during your lifetime have you heard that quote? Does it ring true?

A vital form of the communication process often overlooked is nonverbal communication. It is a powerful tool that helps us to connect with others, express what we really mean and maneuver through difficult situations. Needless to say, nonverbal communication has a significant impact on the overall quality of our relationships, both professionally and personally.

When we interact with others, we continuously send and receive a myriad of wordless cues. Our level of eye contact, the gestures we make, how we walk and sit, other body movements, vocal qualities (tone, pitch, rate, volume, inflection), touch and personal space are all nonverbal behaviors that can send strong messages. These messages can generate a sense of trust, interest and credibility, or they can produce distrust, disinterest and confusion.

" When your verbal message is contradicted by your nonverbal message, you send a mixed message to others."

Keep in mind that when your verbal message (the words you speak) is contradicted by your nonverbal message, you send a mixed message to others. Based on research published in the book, *Silent Messages*, by Dr. Albert Mehrabian, more than 90 percent of the time, the receiver of your mixed message will believe only the nonverbal aspect.

Dane Archer of the University of California at Santa Cruz, in his video series, "Exploring Nonverbal Communication," cites the following as nonverbal elements we should all consider.

• Facial expressions. The human face is extremely expressive, able to convey countless emotions without saying a word. And unlike some forms of nonverbal communication, expressions for happiness, sadness, anger, surprise, fear and disgust are the same across cultures.

• Eye contact. Eye contact is an especially important form of nonverbal communication. The way you look at someone can communicate many things — interest, hostility, attraction, etc. It is also important in gauging the other person's response and in maintaining the flow of conversation. However, you should also be aware of how eye contact is viewed by other cultures.

• Body movements and posture. Consider how your perceptions of people are impacted by the way they walk, sit, slouch, stand up straight or hold their head. The way you move and carry yourself communicates a wealth of information.

87

This includes your posture, bearing, stance and various subtle movements.

• Gestures. They are woven into the very fabric of our daily lives. We wave, point, beckon and use our hands when we're expressing ourselves, often without thinking. However, the meaning of gestures can be very different across cultures and regions, so it's important to be careful to avoid misinterpretation.

• Touch. We communicate a great deal through touch. Think about the messages given by the following: a firm handshake, a timid tap on the shoulder, a warm bear hug, a reassuring slap on the back, a patronizing pat on the head or a controlling grip on your arm.

• Voice. Yes, we actually communicate in a nonverbal manner with our voices. Vocal sounds such as tone, pitch, volume, inflection, rhythm and rate are important nonverbal elements. When we speak, others "read" our voices in addition to listening to our words. These subtle speech sounds provide minute but powerful clues into our true feelings and what we really mean. Think about how tone of voice, for example, can be a sign of anger, sarcasm, affection or confidence.

• Space/proximity. Have you ever felt uncomfortable during a conversation because the other person was standing too close and invading your "personal" space? Well, we all have a need for physical space, although that need differs depending on the culture, the situation and the closeness of the relationship. You can use proximity to communicate many different nonverbal messages, including cues of aggression, dominance, professionalism or affection.

Successful nonverbal communication depends on an understanding of the cues you're sending, coupled with the ability to accurately pick up on the cues others are transmitting to you. When you increase your power in this facet of communication, you will begin to experience improved rapport with and a better understanding of others, which in turn, can certainly lead to expanded trust, confidence and credibility.

People Skills, Enthusiasm Breed Success

(Heard)

Let me begin this piece by declaring that I earned my doctorate in adversity and graduated at the top of my class in the school of hard knocks. As I grow older and, hopefully, wiser, every day becomes more precious than the day before. That's why I try to spend as much time each day reading and learning from others, whether that involves enhancing my skills as a CEO and a trainer or finding new ways of being a better husband, father, grandfather and friend.

Since my formal education was limited, my desire to learn more about God, people and life has always been strong. I've been an avid reader and a student of human nature for decades. Because my wife, Bodi, and I are born-again Christians, we devote a portion of each day to reading our Bible together and discussing what we've learned. Whether or not you are a spiritual person, I strongly recommend that you apply the Golden Rule — do unto others as you would have them do unto you — in your professional and personal lives. No person in the world can succeed as easily and as quickly as one who constantly changes for the better as he learns from both his successes and his failures.

Once we decide to pursue greater peace, happiness and success in our lives, we must strive every day to learn more and to be kinder to others. The old saying that "givers get" can be applied to our everyday lives by developing a habit of giving three kind remarks, three referrals and a smile to the people we encounter on the job and off. In addition, those of us who teach or manage people should know that the more we help others achieve their goals, the more happiness and success we enjoy ourselves. Whether we aspire to become a great leader, a great spouse or parent, or a great salesperson, we must develop the personality for successfully dealing with people.

Years ago, Howard University conducted a study of thousands of people who had been fired from their jobs. It showed that twice as many people had lost their jobs due to failure to deal successfully with people than those who were fired for inability to do the work they had been given. Another study by Dr. Albert Edward Wiggum found that out of 4,000 people who lost their jobs, 90 percent were fired because they hadn't mastered the skill of dealing with people.

In my Alligator Management & Marketing seminars and keynote presentations, I share some of the characteristics of the people we generally prefer to deal with in sales and in life. As buyers, we look for honesty, character, good taste and a track record of success. We also look for someone who is a good listener. Some folks are so mesmerized by the sounds of their own voices that they never learn how to listen to other people or make them feel special. As we look at success in almost any endeavor, we tend to find that in almost every case, the successful person has mastered the skill of dealing with people.

One of the cornerstones of our success at BIC Alliance is that we search long and hard for experts in business and industry to interview and write about in *BIC Magazine*, especially when it comes to writing feature articles about our marketing partners. We go the extra step of finding out what people in industry who have dealt with them have to say about their products, services and reputation. Whether it's buying a car, selecting a doctor or choosing an industrial supplier, it's wise to know what others we know and respect think about them. We take this same approach when we begin work on a new BIC Publishing project. During the development stages of our three books — *Industry Achievers, Energy Entrepreneurs* and *It's What We Do Together That Counts* — we looked for role models who talk the talk and walk the walk when it comes to working hard and being kind to others.

In Les Giblin's book, *How to Have Confidence and Power in Dealing With People*, which was written more than 50 years ago, he relates a quote by the great industrialist Henry Kaiser, who said, "You will automatically practice good human relations if you remember that every individual is important, because everyone is a child of God." The book goes on to say that if we're on good terms with ourselves, we're usually on good terms with others.

> " Whether or not you are a spiritual person, I strongly recommend that you apply the Golden Rule — do unto others as you would have them do unto you."

As the old saying goes, you never get a second chance to make a first impression. Even before we are formally introduced to another person, that individual is sizing us up and creating an impression of us. Perhaps they've heard or read something that cast us in positive or unfavorable light. Our reputation precedes us everywhere we go and in everything we do. We should not, however, allow whatever preconceived notions people have about us to affect how we treat them. If we want others to feel a certain way about us, we've got to begin by thinking differently about them and about what it is we're offering.

Another secret to success centers on enthusiasm. People simply love to be around and deal with others who exude a certain level of enthusiasm for their work or other aspects of their lives. Just think about it. Would you prefer to work with someone who is passionate about his job or someone who hates it? Would you be comfortable buying from someone who really doesn't care about you, the company he works for or the product he's selling? Indifference is contagious, but so are enthusiasm and kindness.

Continuous Slow Improvement the Kaizen Way

(Whitelaw)

"Commit to CANI! — Constant and Never-ending Improvement." — Tony Robbins

I love Tony Robbins. You can see and feel the passion that emanates from this man when he is speaking about self-improvement. Tony loves to talk about CANI. Learning about CANI from Tony is much more entertaining and interesting than the way I learned this stuff. Many years ago as a young DuPont Corp. trainee, I learned all about statistical process control (SPC) and total quality management (TQM) by counting red and white beads. You don't need to be a quality geek like me to understand the true meaning of continuous improvement. All we really need to know is what Oliver Cromwell said many moons ago: "He who stops being better, stops being good."

In the 1950s, "made in Japan" was synonymous with junk. An American quality expert by the name of Dr. W. Edward Deming introduced a war-ravaged nation to the process of continuous improvement. The Japanese understood this concept so well they created their own version, which today is known as Kaizen. When analyzing the word "kaizen," we learn that kai means change and zen means good. The essence of Kaizen is the belief that change is good. Do you have the same belief?

Our world is moving at such a rapid pace that it is difficult to adapt to all the changes. Finding a method to help us adapt is essential for our mental, physical and spiritual survival. There are times when change can trigger the emotion of fear. If we choose to allow change to trigger fear, there is a natural tendency to either fight or flee. If we choose either of these actions, we will not overcome our fears.

Change is an act that will cause most of us to experience an emotion of fear. Have you ever wondered how children describe fear? We often hear children say things like, "I am frightened," "I am scared," or "I am sad" to express their fears. Children sense that they have little control over their world and surroundings, and they say what they feel and think. They frequently adapt to whatever change they encoun-

Ask Small Questions

Think Small Thoughts

Take Small Actions

Solve Small Problems

Bestow Small Rewards

Identify Small Moments

ter and continue to grow by experiencing life. We "big kids" need to learn this lesson.

Adults handle change and fear much differently than children. Adults desire to feel as though they are in control of their world and environment, and, as such, they express fear through anxiety, nervousness, depression or stress. Most adults fail to recognize and accept fear as an emotion. It is easier to fight or flee than to address our fears.

We know that people pay real money to experience fear as the emotion of excitement. Have you ever paid to jump out of an airplane? Some people do. Have you ever paid to get on board a wild and scary amusement park ride? Is there really a difference? Some people are able to turn their fears into a more productive emotion called excitement or adventure. So why can't you? You can!

If you understand that fear is normal and that you can choose another emotion, then Kaizen can help you move past the fear. I like to say that naming the beast

" Our world is moving at such a rapid pace that it is difficult to adapt to all the changes."

is the first step in taming the beast. Kaizen is all about finding and taking small steps toward continuous slow improvement. In Robert Maurer's wonderful book, *One Small Step Can Change Your Life*, he provides us six small steps to help us tiptoe past our fears and accomplish our dreams and goals of all sizes. The six steps are:
- Ask small questions.
- Think small thoughts.
- Take small actions.
- Solve small problems.
- Bestow small rewards.
- Identify small moments.

Ask small questions — Small questions create a mental environment that welcomes unabashed creativity and playfulness. When you ask small questions of others, you can channel that creative force toward team goals. By asking small questions of yourself, you lay the groundwork for a personalized Kaizen program for change.

Think small thoughts — The easy technique of mind sculpture uses small thoughts to help you develop new social, mental and even physical skills just by imagining yourself performing them!

Take small actions — Small actions are at the heart of kaizen. By taking steps so tiny that they seem trivial or even laughable, you'll calmly pass obstacles that have defeated you before. Slowly but painlessly you'll cultivate an appetite for continued success and lay down a permanent new route to change.

Solve small problems — We are so accustomed to living with minor annoyances that it's not always easy to identify them, let alone make corrections. But these annoyances have a way of acquiring mass and eventually blocking your path to change. By training yourself to spot and solve small problems, you can avoid undergoing much more painful remedies later.

Bestow small rewards — Whether you wish to train yourself or others to instill better habits, small rewards are the perfect encouragement. Not only are they inexpensive and convenient but they also stimulate the internal motivation required for lasting change.

The reward should be appropriate to the goal. The reward should be appropriate to the person. The reward should be free or inexpensive.

So how do we put this into action? Let us pretend that we are going to run and complete our first 26.2-mile marathon.

Ask small questions: Whom do I know that has run a marathon before? How do I find out about training for a marathon? Where could I find a local running club that is training for a marathon?

Think small thoughts: Today I am enjoying running a mile in the park. I feel really good, and I am eating well and drinking lots of water. I really enjoy the feel and the look of my new running shoes.

Take small actions: Today I will run 1 mile. I am ordering some new running shoes online. I will plan to eat a healthy breakfast today and drink plenty of water to stay hydrated. I have found a great book on running and will read the first chapter today.

Solve small problems: I need to get up early tomorrow to do a run, so I need to go to bed early tonight. I can't find a running group, but I know some friends who I can run with in the neighborhood. I can't make up my mind about which shoe to buy, so I will ask the owner at the local running store to help me.

Bestow small rewards: I am going to take myself out to dinner to celebrate after I finish my first 10K race. I will reward myself by eating pizza and pasta each night before my long runs. If I complete the half marathon, I will buy a new iPod so I can listen to music when I run.

Implement your success plan one small step at a time using the Kaizen way and nothing will stop you from reaching even your biggest, hairiest, most audacious goals!

Planning Ahead for Career Challenges

(Heard)

One of the great joys that comes from getting older is that most of us tend to become a little wiser. Just think how much more peaceful, happier and successful we might be now if we had known 20, 30 or 40 years ago what we know today.

When you really think about it, life is kind of like a stairway. Assuming that the average lifespan in America today is about 80 years, life can be a stairway of 80 years going either forward or backward. Some folks go forward into peace, happiness and success and others move backward into misery, pain and suffering. While it is impossible to always know what challenges lie ahead of us, we are equipped with the gift of being able to plan ahead for difficult times. For at least one third of my life, I really didn't do much planning when it came to starting a new day, a new week or a new year. By the time most of us reach our late teens and early 20s, however, we realize that planning ahead seems to make things a little better than taking things one day at a time.

As we began the economically turbulent year of 2009, it appeared that many

" It's not how much money we make that counts, but how much we have when we really need it. "

businesses would struggle due to economic instability, leaving many experienced professionals — including executives and managers — searching for new jobs. Whether or not our fates are in our own hands, there are actions we can take to try to strengthen our job security or help us change course if we are forced to move on.

I think back to the lessons I learned as a paid carpenter earning hourly wages more than 40 years ago. In those days, our supervisors would lay off three people every Friday, taking into consideration our work ethic, ability to learn and willingness to follow instructions. Seniority was never a factor. My colleagues and I never knew when we'd get rained out or how long a job would last, so my wife Bodi and I learned to always save a little for the rainy days we knew would come.

I can't help but think about all the folks we know who live from payday to payday and, even worse, those with excellent salaries and years of experience who live above their means and don't have a nest egg set aside. Bodi has stressed to me since our marriage in 1963 that it's not how much money we make that counts, but how much we have when we really need it. So, let this be lesson No. 1 — don't live beyond your means and save something every payday, not only for emergencies but also for opportunities.

I often find myself sharing advice with young industry professionals that I gave to my son-in-law and partner Thomas Brinsko 20 years ago — find great mentors and become active in the professional organizations that serve your industry. Believe it or not, there are industry professionals today who don't take the time out to network with potential customers and colleagues through membership in associations. Enter lesson No. 2 — don't get so busy or think you're so important that you can't stay actively involved with professional organizations in which your customers and peers are involved. I rarely attend a major industry and construction event in Louisiana or Texas where I don't meet the top leaders among buyers and suppliers.

This brings me to lesson No. 3 — give and get great referrals. The best way I know to get excellent referrals — which could prove vital to future job opportunities — is to do a great job where you're presently employed and never take your job security for granted. Not only that, in times of economic challenge, the folks who are the best trained, work the hardest and get along with people the best in their respective companies are most likely to be kept on board. People who have great reputations and excellent networking skills are rarely out of work.

Making a Career Transition: Five Steps to Success

(White)

Changing careers is one of the biggest decisions job seekers can face. Just thinking about the process can be overwhelming. It is a turning point, a time where the changes you make will reshape your career path in a new direction. Keeping this in mind, a career transition usually means a transition in other parts of your life as well, such as additional education/training, relocation or a change in lifestyle.

There are three basic ways to make a career transition. Probably the most difficult way, yet the path many people choose, is to change professions entirely — both the job and the field. Another course to take is to move to a new position in the same industry. And finally, the third option is finding the same position in a new field.

" *The biggest mistake you can make is attempting to change careers without a plan.* "

Almost certainly, the biggest mistake you can make is attempting to change careers without a plan. A successful change may often take months to accomplish when you have a strategy. So, as you might imagine, without a plan you could end up drifting for an even longer period.

There is no "one size fits all" strategy for making a career change. However, there are five fundamental steps to success to consider when making a career transition:

• Determine the "why." Avoid rushing into the change. You should ask yourself what you are seeking to accomplish and why. Do you want to change careers because you dislike your job, your boss or the company culture? Do you want more money/benefits? Try not to confuse disliking your current situation with disliking your overall career. Take the time and effort to analyze whether it's just the job/boss/company that you're not happy with, or whether it's the career/skills/work that you dislike. Whatever you conclude, keep in mind that it's best to maintain your current job, if possible, until you have an action plan in place for finding a new career/job.

• Assess likes and dislikes. Analysis can be a useful activity. It helps us to better understand ourselves. In most cases, determining your dislikes on the job is the easy part. A key question to ask yourself is what do you really like doing when you're at work? What gets you excited and enthused? What do you have

97

a passion for? If you're not quite sure, consider completing a few online career assessments to help you get a better understanding of your "likes." Another option is to visit with a career professional who can administer the appropriate assessments as well as interpret them to best meet your specific needs, and help direct your career transition.

• Research other careers. Examine the possibilities. Avoid jumping into a different career field before you spend some time researching the careers that center on your passion, including fields you may never have considered. Network with your contacts and read career and job profiles. Great career information and skills-matching services can be located via the Internet on Web sites such as www.online.onetcenter.org. The more information you have about various career choices, the more successful you'll be in making a career transition.

• Evaluate transferable skills. Many people already have a good amount of skill and experience that is transferable. Consider your communication skills — oral, written, interpersonal and presentation — and your skills in leadership, planning and organizing, information technology, and customer service. Once again, it's important that you keep in mind the fact that you may need additional education, training or certifications in order to effectively transition into your new career and to enhance your credibility.

• Find a mentor. Changing careers is undoubtedly a challenging undertaking. So, you need to have someone to assist you through the difficult times and help motivate and keep you focused on your goal when you become discouraged. There will be times when the insecurities and lack of confidence set in. When seeking out a mentor, look for someone with whom you can build a relationship, someone who will advise you, someone who has a solid network of contacts, someone who can add to your current level of wisdom and, finally, someone who doesn't just encourage you, but will also be direct and frank with you when you're moving in the wrong direction.

Finding a new job is tough. Making a career transition is even tougher. Yet with a strategic plan and a bit of creativity, you can surely be successful and make it happen.

Assessing Skills is Paramount

(White)

Are you recently laid off and in the need to quickly update your résumé to apply for new job opportunities? Are you considering a career change and in a dilemma as to how to effectively determine your transferable skills needed in today's job market? Looking for resource material that can help get you redirected? Well, not to worry. In this article, I'll bring you a few strategies and resources that can move you forward on the road to success.

It's quite surprising how many people do not fully understand the many skills they can offer an employer. Generally, people either undervalue their skills, or, if they've been doing a particular job for a long time, things come so naturally to them that they aren't aware of all of the skills they use on a daily basis. Research indicates that the average person has more than 500 skills. Unbelievable? Well, you simply need to identify at least five to 10 skills that are the most attractive to potential employers in the job/career of your choosing. So, let's begin the skills brainstorming process.

> *" Research indicates that the average person has more than 500 skills."*

• Determine your technical, nontechnical and transferable skills. Technical skills are those skills specific to a job or occupation. For example, a salesperson's skills would include account management, customer service, contract negotiating, etc. An accountant's skills could include using computer accounting software, preparing taxes, handling accounts payable/receivable, and the list goes on.

• Nontechnical skills are many times referred to as "soft skills or self-management skills"; i.e., a collection of personal qualities, habits and attitudes that make an individual a good employee and compatible to work with. Companies value these skills because research suggests and experience shows that they can be just as important an indicator of job performance as hard or core skills. Examples encompass interpersonal communication skills, teamwork, flexibility/adaptability, problem solving, time management, strong work ethic and ability to accept and learn from constructive feedback.

• Transferable skills, simply put, are the skills you've gathered/acquired through various jobs, volunteer work, hobbies, interests, civic/community/church activities, sports or other life experiences that can be used in your next job or new career.

• Consider skills assessments. *Strengths Finder 2.0* by Tom Rath is a great book that provides an online assessment that enables you to discover your top five talent themes and how they play out/make you stand out in a career, job and life. It's in the $20 range, and I highly recommend this as a great resource to help you further assess your skills. To discover other resources, Google "free online skills assessments," and you'll discover a plethora of materials.

• Reflect on work experience stories. Sound weird? Maybe. Yet, it's a great strategy for discovering skills. Consider situations/tasks you perform on the job; then, think about what skills you have that enable you to do really well. Take for example a customer service scenario — you calmed down a customer and worked with him to get a problem resolved, and he left your office satisfied with your actions. What skills allowed you to accomplish this task? Skills you might consider include active listening, empathizing, conflict management, problem solving and use of appropriate nonverbal cues.

• Network with friends, associates and family. Ask them what skills they see that you have. Many times they'll do a better job of describing your skills than you will.

• Visit online resources. In my opinion, two of the best online career resources you should visit are www.online.onetcenter.org and www.indeed.com. O'Net Center is a comprehensive occupational information Web site. It provides you with free online information regarding job titles and corresponding skills, plus so much more. It's one of my favorites that I consistently recommend. The other Web site, indeed.com, is an aggregate of job opportunities. The site is quite easy to navigate. When you begin your job search, indeed.com is a valuable resource to investigate.

I encourage you to take the time to complete a thorough skills analysis. Make the effort to understand all of the skills you can offer an employer. Begin to think of yourself in terms of your skills rather than just a job title. You will be surprised at the world of career options you had not previously considered for which you would qualify.

Ten Common Job Search Mistakes

(White)

The weak economic environment has created a tough job market. Yet, people are being hired. So, if you're currently in this market, how's your search progressing? "Stalled, stuck in the mud," you say. Well, perhaps this article will shed a bit of light in your tunnel. In my experience as a career coach, résumé writer and consultant, I have witnessed numerous mistakes job seekers make. Below are 10 of the most common mistakes I've seen, coupled with some tips for successfully navigating the search.

1. Lack of commitment. Searching for a job is a job in itself. It's hard work. Applying for a job here and there while hoping for the best, though, is not a winning formula. You need to commit a certain number of hours and do something every day, i.e., connect with someone in your network, search online job boards, research and call companies in your industry, follow up on résumés you've already sent. Most importantly, make a concerted effort to stay positive throughout the process.

2. Failure to network. Think that contacting others will be a burden to them?

" Avoid creating one generic résumé for targeting multiple objectives. "

Absolutely not. Generally, people want to help. Friends, acquaintances, colleagues and others you know can help you develop job leads. You never know when someone will have that perfect lead just for you.

3. Poorly written or designed cover letter and résumé. If your documents are missing the mark, you will not get a callback. Your cover letter should highlight your skill set and strengths that show you are a good match for the job. The résumé should be results-oriented, and show key responsibilities and accomplishments that tune in to the position for which you are applying.

4. One-size-fits-all résumé strategy. Avoid creating one generic résumé for targeting multiple objectives. It is not uncommon in today's job market to have several résumés and cover letters, each customized to a specific position and highlighting the respective accomplishments and key responsibilities.

5. No diversity in your job search. Restricting yourself to online job boards and classified ads can be a huge mistake. Diversify your job search. Consider other effective strategies — networking, recruiters, job fairs, targeted mail contacts with companies, calling employers, etc. And, keep in mind that the old-fashioned method of simply visiting a prospective employer can still be a viable option.

6. Lack of planning and focus. When you fail to plan, you plan to fail. In addi-

tion, with a lack of focus, you may have a difficult time finding a job. Liken the job search to a marketing campaign with you as the product. Focus on the types of jobs in which you are interested, and then develop a game plan that will guide your actions to achieving your goals.

7. Monitoring system nonexistent. Not having a system to track your efforts can cause lots of wasted time. For example, which version of your résumé is getting the most responses? What job search strategy is generating the most interviews? Additionally, keep a log of when résumés were sent, dates of follow-up, callbacks, etc. This process will enable you to observe how your job search is progressing, and to make adjustments as necessary.

8. Ineffective online presence. Are you using Facebook or LinkedIn? If so, how is it working? To enable these social networking Web sites to work for you in the job search process, make sure your information is professional, with relevant material about your strengths and accomplishments in your areas of expertise.

9. Résumé posted at hundreds of job sites. This strategy can certainly be self-defeating. Because you are unable to customize your résumé for a specific job opportunity, your chances of being called can be greatly reduced. It's better to find "niche" sites that relate to your profession/industry. An interesting Web site to try is www.findingjobsonline.com.

10. Poor or no follow-up. Being passive instead of proactive in today's competitive market will not get you the job. As appropriate, follow up with a call or e-mail. Be ready to discuss your interest in the job and the qualifications that make you a good fit.

Searching for a job is generally never easy, regardless of your experience. Yet, knowing some of the mistakes to avoid can help move you in the right direction to conducting a search that can be both successful and rewarding.

Listening — A Key to Interpersonal Success

(White)

During the past year, I have observed that a key misstep many individuals are taking, both professionally and personally, is failing to practice active listening in their everyday interpersonal interactions. In fact, CLI, or "continuous listening improvement," is needed among all age groups.

"To listen effectively is to reach clarity of understanding. To understand clearly is to respond appropriately. To respond appropriately is to enhance communication. To enhance communication is to support cooperation. To support cooperation is to improve morale. To improve morale is to increase job commitment. To increase job commitment is to focus on productivity. Listening is good business!"

The previous quotation from Diana Bonet's book, *The Business of Listening*,

> **"** CLI, or "continuous listening improvement,"
> is needed among all age groups. **"**

is primary evidence that we all need to be good senders as well as good receivers. Isn't it interesting how some of us are so eager to talk, yet so reluctant to listen? The skills needed to improve listening are relatively simple to learn and execute. Perhaps the harder task is developing an active listening attitude. You do this by first understanding that listening is as powerful as speech. What someone says to you can be just as critical as what you have to say to them.

Listening is probably the most important and, yet, the most neglected dimension of communication. How often have you heard these statements: "You're not listening to me." "Why don't you let me finish what I'm saying?" "If you'll only let me, I'll tell you!" "I may as well be talking to a brick wall!" "You just don't understand!" "But that's not what I said!" If you hear any of these comments from others, perhaps it's true that you're not listening. Listening is the art of connecting with another person so you fully understand what they are saying and feeling. It is a vital and necessary skill needed in leading others and maintaining interpersonal relationships in all aspects of our lives.

Did you know people listen about five to 10 times as fast as they speak? In the time it takes the speaker to say 100 words, the listener has the capacity to hear 500-1,000 words. So, while the other person is talking, you may be listening with only a fraction of the capacity for attention. What can you do?

Let's take a look at five keys to active listening:

1. Pay attention. This step enables you to focus. Give the speaker your undi-

vided attention. Stop what you're doing. Maintain good eye contact.

2. Stop talking. Most of us, depending upon the situation, can do two things at once.

Unfortunately, listening is not one of them. You cannot listen when you are also talking. You will only be thinking about what you are going to say next instead of paying attention to what the other person is saying.

3. Be alert to nonverbal cues. Although it is critical to listen to what is being said, it is equally important to understand what is not being said. For example, while a person's verbal message may convey honesty and conviction, his gestures, facial expressions and tone of voice may convey doubt.

4. Avoid interrupting or finishing others' sentences. Interrupting and finishing another's statement can be perceived as disrespectful and suggests you want to do all the talking instead of listening. Be patient. Allow time for the speaker to convey ideas and meaning.

5. Provide feedback. Ask questions and get confirmation and clarification. Examples such as the following can help enhance understanding: "So, you're saying ... " "Let me make sure I understand ... " "Let me see if I'm with you, you ... " "If I heard you correctly, you ... "

Herbert G. Lingren wrote, "I speak because I know my needs/I speak with hesitation because I know not yours/My words come from my life's experiences/Your understanding comes from yours/Because of this, what I say/And what you hear, may not be the same/So, if you will listen carefully/Not only with your ears/But with your eyes and with your heart/Maybe somehow, we can communicate."

Effective listening can be the key to solving problems, reducing conflict, misunderstanding and unpleasantness, as well as enhancing your overall interpersonal communication. Additionally, the payoffs for improving your active listening skills are enormous. You will have fewer communication glitches, your relationships will improve, productivity and morale will increase in your organization, and you will be able to break through those barriers of poor listening to become a more effective and successful communicator professionally as well as personally.

Your Professional Image: Credibility or Crisis?

(White)

Several weeks ago, I conducted a training program for an organization that had recently implemented a new dress code. Though the program went well, many of the organization's employees (those not attending the training, of course) rebelled against the dress code. "Why the need for such a thing?" was the comment of many. In fact, management received feedback regarding the dress code that was unbelievable. Based on the comments, it seemed as though professionalism as it relates to attire and grooming had just about disappeared from that work environment.

It is a fact, based on years of research, that your overall professional image significantly impacts the image of your organization. Unfortunately, there is a profusion of sloppy, unpressed, inappropriate and in-poor-taste attire worn by so

" *Your overall appearance can be your best friend or your worst enemy.* "

many in today's workplace. Perhaps the idea that you never get a second chance to make a first impression has gone by the wayside. So, what is the status of your dress and grooming — one of credibility or one of crisis?

Organizations, both large and small, must be keenly aware that the appearance (attire and grooming) of all employees is directly related to the overall company image and how clients and others perceive the total enterprise. Fortunately, during the past few years, many companies have begun to recognize, again, the power of image and the fact that an employee's individual image can either serve as a positive reflection or a negative one.

Individually, your overall appearance can be your best friend or your worst enemy. At times, clothes are the only visible clues to your personality. Even when other indicators are more apparent, your appearance continues to make a statement. Consider the times when you know that you are dressed appropriately, that you are projecting the type of image the company wants to present. How do you feel? I'll bet that you feel great. Your attitude is positive, self-esteem is high, people have confidence in your ability and judgment, you're less vulnerable to intimidation, and your "look good, feel good" frame of mind comes through in everything you do.

Contrary to popular belief, you don't have to spend a million dollars to be attired professionally and appropriately. Ladies don't need a perfect figure, nor do gentlemen need a perfect physique. What you do need to be concerned about is what is appropriate and in good taste for your specific professional line of work, the type of clothing that compliments your body type and colors that are flattering as well as suitable for the workplace. Most importantly, you should be willing to change, coupled with the desire put your "best self" forward in every situation.

In general, a quick check in the mirror each day should be enough to tell you if you're on the right track. If you look like you're dressed to go somewhere other than to your job, you probably aren't dressed appropriately for work. Also, ask what messages the clothes you are wearing will send. If your response is "not really professional and in good taste," perhaps you should go back to your closet and change.

The way you dress, how you're groomed, your overall demeanor — these factors taken together are your visual communication. When you're dressed inappropriately, the fight for credibility is so much harder. Consider that your appearance "talks." Many times your dress and grooming are speaking so loudly that others have difficulty listening to what you have to say. Bear in mind that your look of confidence, of competence and of credibility can give you the opportunity to demonstrate your capabilities. As Shakespeare once said, "the apparel oft proclaims the man."

When it's all said and done, the bottom line is that a well-polished image gives you a psychological and competitive edge and earmarks you as a professional. I certainly hope you agree with me when I say that one of the most important goals of a professional is to, indeed, look like one.

Seal the Deal With a Meal

(White)

The purposes of business entertaining are numerous. You can strengthen business relationships; woo clients; seal a major deal; or discuss details of projects, proposals and contracts. When you add good food to the occasion, the potential for goodwill is heightened.

Wheeling and dealing over breakfast, lunch or dinner has become a highly successful and popular way of doing business. Whether the occasion runs three hours with the accompanying tab hitting the $100-plus mark or consists of half an hour over a cup of coffee, pizza or a hamburger, don't underestimate the value of sitting down over a meal to hammer out a business deal or build a relationship prior to discussing business. On the other hand, never underestimate how devastating not being able to properly handle that lunch or dinner can be.

Any type of business entertainment creates a situation in which all of your social graces and skills should come together, from your table manners and abili-

> *" Any type of business entertainment creates a situation in which all of your social graces and skills should come together."*

ties as a host to your communication skills.

With that in mind, we will review a few basic guidelines for planning a breakfast, lunch or dinner. These guidelines will help make the experience more pleasant and profitable for you and your clients.

Planning the meal

With the old saying, "Prior planning prevents poor performance," goes another truism: "Planning ahead and making proper arrangements eliminates the risk of disappointment, confusion and missed opportunities." Any planning you do in advance of the business meal will ease your job once you get to the restaurant and will make you and your guests better able to relax, enjoy the meal and close the deal.

When making arrangements, let the person invited check his calendar for the best date, then decide on a mutually satisfactory date and time. Always confirm arrangements a day or two before the meeting. When choosing the restaurant, ask your guest for his preference. If the choice of restaurant is left to you, it is generally a good idea to choose one with which you are familiar. Time constraints and location should also be kept in mind when making your decision.

107

If you wish to try a new restaurant, call in advance to check on reservation policies, prices, hours of service, proximity of tables and types of food served. When making reservations, give your full name and the name of your company. To avoid embarrassment at the end of the meal, make it clear to restaurant personnel that you will be paying the bill.

Consider the situation

Should you find yourself hosting business meals with any regularity, it is a good idea to frequent a certain restaurant and establish rapport with the owner or the maître d'.

They will see that you are seated at a good table for business discussions and that your service is top-notch. In addition, being welcomed at the restaurant by the owner or others will impress your business guests.

Whether your guest is from out of town or around the corner, never exceed your budgetary constraints. No business deal was ever consummated simply because someone took a client to the most expensive restaurant in town. Be aware that many restaurants have luncheon specials and special dinner menus with modestly priced meals. It is a good idea to call ahead of time and inquire about these menus, as well as whether or not you need to make reservations during the times these special meals are offered.

If your guests have been on the road for an extended period of time or have just come a long distance to meet with you, have pity on their physical condition. They may have had travel delays and other problems. Don't take obviously exhausted persons to a noisy restaurant where it is difficult to talk, much less think.

Also, consider the day of the week. It would be naive to request a quiet dinner, even at better restaurants, on a Friday or Saturday evening. A peaceful evening spent over a quiet dinner is much more conducive to the successful transaction of business.

Keep in mind the restaurant selected will be perceived as an extension of your office. Be precise about the time and place to meet. Should it be necessary to meet in a crowded place, suggest a spot that is both secure and comfortable. If this is a first-time meeting, give detailed information. Guests will feel more confident about finding you without the embarrassment of approaching the wrong person.

Plan to arrive for the meeting a few minutes ahead of time. A good host greets his guests; his guests greet the poor host. When being led into the dining room by the maître d', guests should precede the host and follow the maître d'. If seating themselves, the host should take the lead. When awaiting guests at the table, the host should not eat bread nor order a drink before their arrival. Be sure to leave the guests' names at the reservation desk.

The host should take charge of the seating arrangements. Everyone can be put at ease by directing each guest to an appropriate seat. When approaching the table with guests, make sure they are seated first.

There are some inviolable rules of seating. When two people are dining at a square table, they should sit next to each other at a right angle. Talking from positions directly across the table can be possibly construed as confrontational or intimidating, and hearing may be difficult.

When hosting two business associates, the more senior partner should be invited to sit directly opposite the host, and have the junior person sit on the right of a left-handed person and on the left of a right-handed person. Avoid placing guests on either side, because it will feel like being a spectator at a tennis match.

Moderate imbibing has become an accepted part of today's business lunches and dinners. What isn't acceptable is heavy drinking. A drink before lunch or dinner may be a formality that lends an air of informality to a potentially tense situation; but ordering three drinks, whether the guest or the host, can spell disaster. As host, ask what the guests will have, then order the drinks for them. As a nondrinking host or guest, I recommend — rather than ordering nothing at all — asking for sparkling or mineral water, cranberry juice or any number of nonalcoholic beverages available. This helps keep those who are drinking from feeling uncomfortable.

When the server comes for the order, as the host, have the guests' selections taken first. As a guest, don't order an appetizer unless invited to do so. If the host suggests wine, let him order. Order dessert or after-dinner drinks only if urged or if the host does. If there is no limit on what can be ordered, the host might say, "I'm not sure I will have much, but please order whatever you like," or, "I'm very hungry today. I hope you are, too."

At any meal, the host should wait until all guests have been served before partaking of a cocktail, sipping the wine or taking a bite of food. However, if time is of the essence, the host should encourage everyone to begin eating when served.

A few helpful hints on table manners to consider:

• As a guest, always watch the host and follow his cues for everything from where to sit to when it is time to leave.

• After being seated, wait to see if the server will unfold the napkin. If he does not, unfold it to a comfortable size (traditionally in half for a large napkin and opened completely for a small napkin).

• If the need arises to leave the table during the meal, excuse yourself, fold the napkin neatly and place it to the left of the plate. If the napkin is particularly soiled, place it in your chair.

• It is important to remember that everything of importance is to the right. For example, the guest of honor sits to the right of the host; food is passed to the right.

• Never be intimidated by the presence of several pieces of flatware. The utensils are arranged in the order in which they will be used. Use them from the outside in.

• Never sprinkle salt and pepper over the food without tasting it first; this is considered an insult to the chef. Also, don't request catsup for anything other than a hamburger and fries. Once again, it is insulting to the chef to use this condiment on well prepared, quality meat or fowl.

• Break off one piece of roll at a time, and butter each piece as it is eaten. Don't put bread on the table by the plate. It should go on the dinner plate or bread plate, if available.

• When eating soup, spoon it toward the rear of the bowl. This way, any drips will fall into the dish. If the last drop in the bottom of the bowl is wanted, tilt the bowl away and spoon it out. When finished, rest the soup spoon in the bowl if it is large, or on the plate or saucer beneath the bowl.

• The rule for finger foods, which ones are and which ones aren't, and how to deal with them vary from one section of the country to another. A sensible rule of thumb: If it looks as though it can be eaten with the fingers, go ahead; if uncertain, eat it with a knife and fork. As a guest, follow the host's lead.

While this may seem like a great deal to remember, don't worry – it can be done. A little practice always helps.

New Study Shows Happiness is Contagious

(Voss)

Well, duh! You and I already know that but now so do some researchers*. The doctors studied 4,739 participants from 1983 through 2003. They reported that the happiness state of mind even extended to the happy person's spouse, friends and neighbors, too.

Here's something else from a separate study, "Healthy people might be happier; and people who are happy and satisfied with their lives might be healthier." Duh again. Haven't we already learned that a positive attitude aids the healing process, reduces stress and helps build the immune system? It is also proven that those with a positive attitude tend to live longer than those who have a mostly apathetic or negative outlook.

Who wouldn't want to be around someone who is generally upbeat, optimistic and forward looking?

Workplace happiness

So how does a "happy state of mind" affect your business? Happy workers tend to be more resilient. They are able to adapt to market changes and can handle

" A positive attitude aids the healing process, reduces stress and helps build the immune system."

customer problems/complaints better. When organizations are generally happy, employee retention is maximized and productivity is higher.

Dr. Tim Sharp, an Australian Clinical Psychologist and Organizational Psychology expert, works with business executives to teach them how to motivate workers and generally create a "happy" or more positive business atmosphere. According to Dr. Sharp, "People operate at their best when they are happy with their work. They collaborate and communicate with colleagues better. They are less likely to get sick. All of this improves the bottom line."

Happiness can be learned

"Happy talk" doesn't mean that we deny reality or we turn a blind eye to problems. It doesn't mean that we won't get sick. But it does mean that we can alter our perception and attitude about problems. Dr. Sharp says, "We can't control what we have to do but we can control how we think about what we have to do and how we approach it. So instead of thinking, 'This flu has really gotten

111

me down,' think of all the days of wellness you've enjoyed and know that this is temporary. Let the sick days run their course and vow to appreciate the well days even more in the future. If you don't like your current job, think of it as a learning experience or as a stepping-stone to a better future."

Some workers have particularly tough jobs such as those who care for the old, sick and dying. A Canadian study measured two groups of long-term healthcare workers who worked with aging patients. One group received coaching on how to change their attitude about their patients and the true importance of what they did, while the second group received no training.

The coached group saw an increase of 23 percent when it came to teamwork, a 10-percent increase in job satisfaction and a 17-percent jump in workplace morale. (The employer saved $12,000 in five months due to a decrease in employee absenteeism.)

Gratitude and forgiveness

Many members of the clergy stress the importance of gratitude and forgiveness as they relate to happiness. Gratitude is the same as counting one's blessings. Forgiveness is the decision to let go of resentful thoughts (carrying a grudge eats into contentment).

"When you don't practice forgiveness, you may be the one who pays most dearly," says Katherine M. Piderman, Ph.D., staff chaplain at the Mayo Clinic in Rochester, Minn. "By embracing forgiveness you embrace peace, hope, gratitude and joy."

Why would someone in advertising/marketing give a whit about happiness in the workplace? It's because good advertising can attract a customer, but to keep them, it takes a well-managed, well-honed organization that's healthy in all areas including production, customer services, customer retention and employee retention.

Happiness is one component of productivity (profit) while pessimism/ negativity is costly. The U.S. Department of Labor estimates that negativity in the workplace costs about $3 billion annually. So to you executives, supervisors, managers and workers, isn't it time to get serious about getting happy? Pessimism costs, while a positive attitude — from the top down and the bottom up — makes everyone in the organization happier. If happiness is catching, then catch all you can.

* Nicholas A. Christakis, M.D., Ph.D., M.P.H., of Harvard and James H. Fowler, Ph.D., of the University of California San Diego conducted the study.

Stimulate Your Job Satisfaction

(White)

How's your level of job satisfaction? Is it positive or negative? Are you in a funk? Do you find yourself humming the Rolling Stones' famous refrain, "I can't get no satisfaction"?

In the 2006 General Social Survey conducted by the National Opinion Research Center at the University of Chicago, 47 percent of those surveyed across all occupations said they were satisfied with their jobs. The survey was based on interviews with randomly selected people who collectively represent a cross section of Americans. Interviewers asked more than 27,000 people questions about job satisfaction and general happiness.

Tom Smith, director of the General Social Survey, states in a published report on the study, "Work occupies a large part of each worker's day, is one's main source of social standing, helps to define who a person is and affects one's health

" You can change your current circumstances by changing your attitude about them."

both physically and mentally." Smith goes on to say that "because of work's central role in many people's lives, satisfaction with one's job is an important component in overall well-being."

The survey points out that the top 10 most satisfying jobs are mostly professions involving caring for, teaching and protecting others, and creative pursuits. The least satisfying jobs are mostly low-skill, manual and service occupations, especially involving customer service and food/beverage preparation and serving.

So, where do you stand? Are you in the 47 percent of workers who are experiencing job satisfaction, or are you in the 53 percent who are dissatisfied? Whatever your position, here are three considerations to help stimulate your level of job satisfaction. I highly recommend that you get a pad and pencil and take notes.

1. Determine what you like about your job. First of all, job satisfaction describes how content you are with your job. What establishes satisfaction on the job for you? Is it the job itself? The people with whom you work? The opportunity to utilize the skills you enjoy most in performing tasks? Your manager's leadership style? The company's organizational culture? The level of contribution or sense of accomplishment you are experiencing? Or, perhaps, it's the money and benefits? I encourage you to think long and hard. This exercise can

be an eye-opener.

2. Determine what you don't like about your job. Of course, it's easy to simply reverse some of the factors previously stated. However, there are other considerations. Are you in a rut? Is your job no longer challenging? Perhaps, because of the time you spend on the job, you are in the throes of a work-life imbalance. Once again, carefully think about the specifics that cause you angst on your job.

3. Evaluate your current job potential. Are there opportunities for advancement, a lateral transfer or job enhancement? A question you need to ask yourself at this stage is, "Can I love the job I'm with, or do I need to move on?" Keep in mind, though, that the grass is not always greener on the other side. Can you get what you need elsewhere? With the state of the economy, what is the job market in your geographic locale for your area of expertise? I certainly suggest that you do your research well before you decide to take the leap.

With all things considered, maybe you should just develop a positive outlook on things. Generally, you can change your current circumstances by changing your attitude about them. Developing an optimistic point of view and changing negative self-talk patterns can be helpful, reduce stress and add to your overall productivity.

In addition to determining what you like about your job and what you dislike, assess your current state of mind. You may need to make some changes in yourself to see things in a more positive light. Whatever your needs, going through this thought-provoking process can certainly help you to make a more informed decision.

Making Work Fun

(Heard)

One day while scanning a dictionary, I ran across the word "laugh." I stopped to read more because just that morning, I was talking to my partner and son-in-law Thomas about the importance of enjoying life and the joy of laughter both at work and at home.

One of our main criteria at BIC Alliance is not only to do a good job, but to have fun while doing it. There is no more uplifting feeling when I'm at work at my desk than to hear laughter among our staff members in another part of the building.

Laughter — that lyrical manifestation of unbridled joy — is one of the greatest gifts the Creator has bestowed upon us. Laughter makes the tedious less burdensome, the foreboding less gloomy and the distressing less worrisome.

I have known some folks who take life so seriously that I rarely, if ever, hear them laugh. Believe it or not, I know a few people whose only laughter is nothing

" I believe that even poor jobs can become better jobs with a positive attitude."

more than an occasional smirk.

I can think of nothing sadder than encountering someone who does not know the utter exhilaration of simple, heartfelt laughter. Many people just don't know how to laugh. They never learned to laugh at life's little pecadilloes, at the sometimes dubious twists of fate, or perhaps most importantly, at themselves.

Some seem to laugh only for all the wrong reasons. How many people do you know who laugh only when being rude or condescending to others? How many find their amusement in the misfortunes of others?

I learned long ago not to take life too seriously, and that when it comes down to a choice between laughter or tears, laughter wins every time.

Making work fun is important — more so than many of us realize.

To most, having fun means laughter, liveliness, merriment and giving joy and pleasure to others. Of course, making money the old-fashioned way through honest, hard work can also be fun. Whether working in an industrial plant, on a drilling rig, at a construction site or in a corporate office, it can be immensely satisfying and enjoyable to deliver a quality product or service.

One of the best examples of a successful "fun" company is Southwest Airlines. Southwest has been selected No. 1 in the airline industry on many occasions and has been named one of the best companies to work for in America.

Southwest founder Herb Kelleher is one person who believes that work, business and fun should go hand in hand. If you believe in reading for fun and profit, I strongly recommend *Nuts!*, which is the amazing success story of Southwest Airlines. When I met Herb Kelleher in 1993, I was struck by how down-to-earth he was and how much fun he was to be around. Kelleher's joie de vivre carries over into the Southwest staff, making it one of the most enjoyable airlines on which to travel.

We have tried to instill the "work is fun" attitude at BIC Alliance, both for our clients and staff members. We endeavor to make our marketing campaigns, trade show and conference participation, and other services as much fun as possible.

Enjoying your job is extremely important not only to your performance at work but also to your entire approach to life. If you like your job, it can be the best job in the world.

What is the best job in the world? If we ask 100 people, we would surely get 100 different answers.

Surely clergymen feel they have the best job in the world, helping the members of their congregations in their search for salvation. Doctors, nurses, policemen and firefighters must feel the same about their professions — saving lives and helping prevent crime.

I believe that your attitude toward your job helps make it the best job in the world. If you find your work fulfilling, if you contribute not only to your livelihood, but to the good of others as well, what could be better?

You see, it's all a matter of perspective. The best job in the world means different things to different people, just as it means different things at different times to each of us. Too often we concentrate on the negative aspects of our jobs rather than accentuating the positive. However, I believe that even poor jobs can become better jobs with a positive attitude.

How to Create a 'Mind Map'

(Whitelaw)

A couple of years ago I was watching my daughter, Tori, write down some notes taken from her history book. Her notes were different from the ones I used to create in school. She used different colored pencils to draw pictures, circles of key concepts, dates and events. I inquisitively asked Tori if this was some type of school art project. She told me it was simply a way of summarizing a large amount of information on one page in the form of a "mind map." Her teacher had instructed the class on how to create mind maps for the purpose of retaining and retrieving the essential information being taught and learned. A few weeks later, Tori showed me the "A" she had received on her AP history test and I began to wonder if this was a technique that I could successfully employ in my job and in my studies.

I don't know about you, but no one taught me how to take notes utilizing a mind map while in school, but I wish they had. Through years of reading and self-study, I too, have learned that creating a mind map is a fun, fast and highly efficient way of taking notes and capturing information. A mind map is nothing more than a highly visual set of colorful diagrams. Mind mapping is a right-

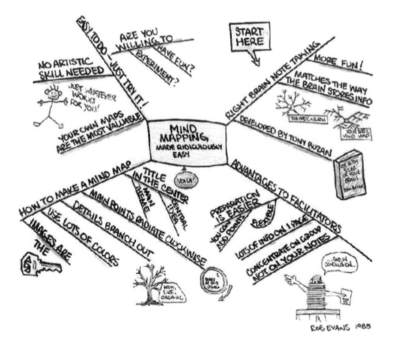

117

brained note-taking technique developed by Tony Buzan and others over the past several decades.

The technique mirrors the way our mind works by linking ideas through branches of association, rather than linear logic. Mind mapping utilizes our visual memory and spatial memory, allowing us to access the most powerful memory centers of the brain. The advantages of this technique over outlining and other more traditional ways of taking notes is that it appears to more successfully integrate retention of essential information in our brain. I also find it to be a lot more fun and interesting way to learn.

My friend, Rob Evans, is an expert in the use of mind maps, and he uses this tool to facilitate high-level discussions and resolve complicated issues. He finds that the process is more flexible than an outline and allows him to easily go back and add points without disrupting the basic map structure or group flow. The technique allows lots of information to be put on one page in a stimulating, organized and creative way. Evans finds that working from a mind map allows him to focus more attention upon the group he is facilitating, thereby permitting

" Creating a mind map is a fun, fast and highly efficient way of taking notes and capturing information."

a more expeditious accomplishment of the task at hand.

Mind maps are easy to make and easy to read. Evans suggests these simple guidelines:

• The title, main theme or central idea is located in the middle of the page.

• Main points radiate from the center, beginning at 1 o'clock and going clockwise.

• Sub-points and other details branch off the main limbs from the center outward.

• It helps to use at least two different colors for the main limbs, alternating them to keep these areas separate from each other.

• Use images and pictures to make the concepts come alive.

Other people's mind maps may be interesting, but the most valuable ones are those you create for yourself. You don't need artistic ability, just a willingness to experiment and to have fun. A few graphical tricks go a long way.

I have found that mind mapping is a great planning and scheduling tool. I use it to organize my thoughts as I prepare to write *BIC Magazine* articles, plan daily work activity, summarize books I have read, plan business or personal trips, and take notes at seminars and meetings. It is a fantastic tool for brainstorming, and for me, an essential tool utilized in a wide array of business activities. Perhaps you will also be able to better understand the notes you have taken when reviewed shortly thereafter or when you wish to revisit them many years later.

I suggest that the next time you want help bringing more information "to light from your mind" on a specific subject, simply draw a circle in the center of a piece of paper and write the following question: "What else do I know about _____?" Then, build a mind map with the thoughts flowing from your mind, relative to the question asked. You will unquestionably be amazed at how much information is hidden in your mind — just awaiting release vis-à-vis this technique.

Building Better Relationships for Success On the Job and Off

(Heard)

The Golden Rule can be taken one step further by helping others accomplish their goals and ambitions. How do we make others feel special and want to respond in kind? The answer is simple — stop, look and listen. People who care genuinely about others know that one of the greatest compliments you can give to another person is the simple courtesy of listening.

In this "Superman" world of ours, we're trying constantly to be faster than a speeding bullet. Most of us don't stop long enough to examine ourselves, much less others. Self-reflection is key when we're trying to improve our lives and those of others. After all, as the Bible says, we cannot look at a splinter in another person's eye without first removing the plank in our own. We must ask ourselves what things we want most out of life. A better relationship with God? More money, more friends and a promotion? Better relationships with our spouses, relatives and friends? More free time or job security?

> *" Once we master the art of 'stop, look and listen,' our lives get better on the job and off."*

Research has taught us that, along with survival, recognition is one of man's greatest needs. How can we do a better job of recognizing others? The answer is simple — we learn to stop and look at their lives with empathy and listen attentively to what they have to say. I learned long ago that how effectively we stop, look and listen can not only save our lives, it can make them better.

Think back to when you were a child learning how to cross the street for the first time. You were likely told to stop walking, look both ways and listen for sounds of oncoming cars before proceeding. In every training session I've conducted since I was a teenage lifeguard teaching others how to swim, I've begun by emphasizing the importance of the "stop, look and listen" approach. Once we master the art of "stop, look and listen," our lives get better on the job and off. How many of us have been told by our spouses, children or fellow employees that we don't listen? We all know people who tend to not listen very well, but it's an easy skill to master — the more we practice, the better we get. A great place to practice is at home with your family.

121

Improving the Supervisor/Subordinate Relationship

(Heard)

The success of any company depends on its most vital resource — people. How well the people in the organization cooperate and pull together determines the degree of its ultimate success. As a supervisor or a subordinate, you can contribute to that success with an understanding of the relationships that exist between you and those with whom you interact.

To improve your ability to work with supervisors, it is beneficial to know what management expects, how to sell your ideas and how to stay on the "right side."

" How well the people in an organization cooperate and pull together determines the degree of its ultimate success."

Following are some of the tasks that a supervisor expects of personnel in just about any field:
- Complete a job on time while controlling quality and costs.
- Keep up with technological developments in a specific field of expertise.
- Make sound decisions rather than waiting for management to make them.
- Plan, organize, control and coordinate the work of subordinates.
- Know and apply company policies and procedures.
- Handle employee and customer complaints properly, while knowing how to prevent complaints from occurring.
- Improve procedures and gain employees' acceptance of them.
- Build cooperation and morale among other employees.
- Communicate within the company or organization effectively and honestly.
- Accept criticism and use it to improve job performance.
- Be ready to handle crises and emergencies but work to prevent their occurrence.

The manner in which ideas are presented to your boss (and the time to decide to share them) has a lot to do with their acceptance. First of all, choose a time when the boss will be able to invest in listening to your idea. Also, be cognizant of your company's financial standing when presenting an idea that requires an expense. Here are some more suggestions:
- State the idea very clearly, whether verbally or in writing.

- Estimate the value of the idea. Project figures if applicable.
- List the pros and cons of the concept.
- Show how and where the idea will fit into the company.
- Be willing to compromise when it comes to implementation of your idea.

Some of the indicators you can look for when asking, "How do I rate with the boss?" are affirmative answers to the following questions. Does the boss ask for your opinion? Does he let you take care of your subordinates? Does he give you constructive criticism? Does he back you up?

Of course, the first step is to know what the boss expects. Beyond that, here are a few other suggestions for keeping in good standing:
- Cooperate fully with one's immediate superior — obey his orders and carry out his instructions. Support his efforts; do not "stab him in the back."
- Report the outcome of any important phase of the job completely and accurately.
- Display courtesy and respect to the boss at all times. He may be difficult to like as a person, but remember that he is the boss. Disrespect will not improve the situation.
- Always assume full responsibility for work assigned to you and your employees. Don't pass the buck if anything goes wrong.
- Stay out of trouble with clients or other departments. Avoid petty bickering with other supervisors. This only creates problems that the boss will have to resolve. Don't add to his workload.

Incorporate the above suggestions into your performance, and you'll see an improvement in both your work and your relationship with the boss.

Controlling Anger, Managing Stress and Staying Calm Under Pressure

(Heard)

Over the years, I've had to end business relationships with people because of anger. Some have allowed their wrath to prompt them to resign. Others have had to be terminated because they couldn't get along with their colleagues.

Ending a hostile relationship with an angry person is like removing a cancer from the lives of both parties. It's the same way, perhaps even better, when we commit ourselves to removing anger from our own lives.

We must strive to live more harmoniously with others. We must practice patience and empathy. We must lead by example and train ourselves and those around us to do the same. When we make mistakes, we should apologize.

One of the best ways to prevent agitation from becoming anger is to confront the situation, discuss it with whomever you are having a problem and work together for a peaceful solution. Of course, the time to confront the situation is when emotions have subsided.

" While we cannot keep negative thoughts from entering our mind, we can determine how long they remain and what thoughts we replace them with."

We can help make our relationships, our professions and our lives happier, healthier and more prosperous by thinking before we speak, speaking softly, taking the time to sleep on important decisions and remembering to confront negative situations at the right time in the right way. When we make mistakes, we should apologize. In my mind, the six most important words related to conflict resolution are "I'm sorry, it won't happen again."

Remember, people may forget what we say or do, but they will always remember how we make them feel.

The inner smile and mind control

Years ago, I made a training film about job burnout. Many of the techniques included in that program were drawn from my personal experiences in industry dealing with large groups of people such as unions and other professional organizations. Stress can make a person mentally and physically tired and far less productive, leading to poor performance or, in industrial settings, accidents that cause injury or even death. The way I learned to deal with this long ago is through a combination of the "inner smile" and mind control. I guess you could call this "Devil Management" because I think that anytime we allow negative thoughts or negative people to linger in our minds, it is the work of the Devil and must be controlled by immediately taking that negative thought and trying to turn it into a positive thought.

I use this method in confrontational situations, including management disputes and handling sales objections. I start by putting on an outer smile that helps me transform my inner feelings into that inner smile. While we cannot keep negative thoughts from entering our mind, we can determine how long they remain and what thoughts we replace them with.

Another technique that utilizes the same concept is developing a "to do" list each day, even when I'm not working. For years, my wife Bodi would feel overwhelmed any time she had five or more things to do. Nowadays, however, she develops a "to-do" list any time she begins to feel overloaded or overwhelmed. Personally, I prefer to use a day-timer for this purpose instead of a cell phone or a computer because I feel more comfortable having a hard copy right in front of me at all times. Another important component of stress management and mind control is giving yourself short-term and long-term rewards. This can be as simple as stopping for a Coke or a glass of water after achieving a certain task (making a set number of sales calls, for instance) or going to dinner to reward yourself for a closing a sale.

During my time in the Army Reserve and in the business of industrial fire and safety, I learned that we must acquire the ability to reprogram our thinking to replace stress with recollection of skills we obtained during training or time spent with mentors. I would say it probably took me about five years in industry and another three to five years in management to really refine my crisis management skills and develop sound mind control and temper management techniques. Anger and stress management, of course, are lifetime processes.

The day I knew I had arrived was when our executive management team did a survey of all the employees in our division at Ethyl Corp. about why every employee chose a particular general foreman's shift over others. My shift went from being the last shift filled to the first because the men said they always knew where they stood with me and that they felt they were the safest in a crisis when working with me. As my skill in this area improved, I became recognized as the go-to guy when a fire or explosion broke out. The key is to be able to take these skills and use them in our personal lives to remain calm and collected in our family lives and in the business sector to make money and deal with adversity and rejection.

If you really think about it, stress management is all about mindset. We must have the ability to see adversity as a blessing that enables us to become better and stronger. It is a blessing when young folks either achieve that ability or learn those skills at a fast rate. From a personal evaluation standpoint I believe anyone who can do it before the age of 30 is exceptional. I also think anyone over 50 who doesn't have that perspective may need to try a little harder or else they may never get it. But we're never too old to see the light!

126

The Courtesy Phenomenon

(Heard)

A few years ago a young sales executive visited our Baton Rouge office for a crash course in strategic marketing. Before leaving, the young lady asked me to share with her in a nutshell the keys to management and sales success. My responses were immediate — hard work, perseverance, learning, networking, asking questions and being courteous to everyone you meet, all the time. Courtesy, for instance, is one of the best investments that you can make in your business or personal life.

Stop and think about it for a minute — I'll bet that you can remember instantly not only the most courteous people you know but also the companies whose employees treat you with the most courtesy.

Of all the compliments we receive here at BIC Alliance, none is appreciated more or received more often than "Your folks are great to work with. They're all so nice, professional and courteous!"

> " I believe lack of courtesy has caused more people to lose promotions than lack of knowledge."

In any organization, courtesy begins at the top and spreads like wildfire. The greatest manager I ever worked for was Merlin Keonecke, plant manager of Ethyl Corp., more than 30 years ago. Mr. Keonecke was one of the most soft-spoken, courteous men I've ever met. His skill was management by walking around and asking questions. Every morning he would walk several miles, say hello to several hundred employees and stop in every plant to ask questions not only to managers but also to craftsmen, operators and contractors. He would always begin with a courteous hello and ask how we were doing, how our families were doing and how things were going in our units. Then he'd ask questions about specific things, i.e. rates, safety operations and maintenance problems.

When one of us couldn't answer a question that we were expected to know, Mr. Keonecke didn't raise his voice, criticize us or use profanity — his nonverbal cues were enough to let us know he was disappointed. Sometimes he'd say he was disappointed and that he expected us to have a better handle on things.

Once any of us experienced Mr. Keonecke's disappointment, we made it a point never to disappoint him again. By the time our plantwide meetings took place at 9 a.m., Mr. Keonecke had a better feel for the entire operation than every individual plant manager in the facility. And when we did something special he always made a point of recognizing us individually. He was loved by everyone, and our plant ran better under his watch than at any other time during my 15 years at Ethyl. I developed my management style more from Mr. Keonecke than anyone I know and am still trying to match his excellence after three decades.

It's important to note that being courteous involves more than good manners. It also includes mastering the art of listening, proper telephone etiquette and treating others the way you'd like to be treated. When Bodi and I stay at a hotel or eat at a restaurant, how the people treat us is more important than the quality of the room or the taste of the food.

Perhaps that's why we really enjoy working with people in the hospitality and travel industries — for the most part, they're more hospitable than people in other industries. In the energy business, most people are courteous, but some have a long way to go.

One interesting thing I've noticed is that folks who are "on the way up" in their professional lives are often less courteous than their supervisors and managers. Several years ago, I was planning to do a feature story about one of the South's top destinations for visitors. The person in charge of marketing and communications for that particular destination was so rude and condescending that we decided to feature an entirely different place. Personally, I believe lack of courtesy has caused more people to lose promotions than lack of knowledge. In my own life, I know for a fact that I've accomplished more by being nice than I have by being smart.

So how do we change a lifetime of habits in one day? Start off one day at a time and try to be as courteous as you can each day. Try to say one nice thing to at least three people who deserve it each day, and observe their responses. Try saying "please" and "thanks" throughout the day, and "I'm sorry" when appropriate, and watch what happens. As you find life getting better and people enjoying your company more, you might even venture into uncharted territory like smiling regularly, letting folks out in traffic, returning phone calls, listening attentively or even sending a thank-you card or e-mail.

Once you've proved to yourself that this attitude is effective, try spreading courtesy throughout your company and your family. Just imagine a world where everyone, including our fellow citizens, spouses and children, were courteous to one another. You may be part of a new courtesy epidemic that spreads across America and around the world.

Well, it may take a while to spread around the entire world, but in a few weeks it can spread around the world in which most of us live.

But isn't that a great place to start?

Ten Tips to Win Again and Again

(Heard)

Experts tell us that we are 50-75 percent more likely to achieve a goal simply by writing it down and reviewing it often. So, do you have a set of business and personal goals already written down? If not, why not start today? For those who haven't laid out a game plan for winning, I'll share a few tips that have worked for me over the years.

1. First and foremost, make God, family and others first in your life. I have tried going it alone and failed over and over. When I started making God, family and others first, my life turned around for the better. Remember that you can't out give God and when you make God No. 1, he will respond in kind. As for family, the greater husband, father and relative we strive to be, the better our family life will be. Just imagine if all of us treated God and our family better than we do our best client. The same is true for mankind — the more we strive to help those less fortunate, the better we will feel about ourselves. The better we feel, the better we do.

> *" Experts tell us that we are 50-75 percent more likely to achieve a goal simply by writing it down and reviewing it often."*

2. Have a plan. Write down your business and personal accomplishments near the end of each calendar year, and write down your goals for the next year.

3. Practice "The People Secret." Les Giblin is one of my favorite sages when it comes to finding a more peaceful, happier and successful life on the job and off. His people secret is really simple — make others No. 1. When you make others No. 1 they tend to realize how wise we are, and they will respond in kind. The best two ways I know to make others No. 1 are to say one nice thing to at least three people a day, and make at least three referrals a day. Remember, givers get — when you help others get what they want, they will be more likely to help you.

4. Do right! These two words can make all the difference in how well our life goes. Just imagine how much better Tiger Woods' life would be right now if he'd just done right. None of us is perfect, but that doesn't mean we can't strive for perfection. We all have a moral compass that tells us what is right and what isn't. We can never go wrong when we do right.

5. Be a mentor and a protégé. Never stop learning from or training others. None of us is the best at everything. Find mentors who excel in the areas you

want to improve in and seek their counsel and advice. Also, become a mentor to others who are less experienced; the more folks you help climb the ladder of success, the more folks will be helping you climb up with them.

6. Be prepared. The more we learn the more we earn. Some folks are great at preparing for crises but don't put the same effort in preparing for success. Be prepared for both.

7. Know yourself, your industry, your company and your competition. The better we evaluate ourselves the more we know about our strengths and short-comings. Write down your strengths and weaknesses and then focus on improvement. The same is true about knowing our industry, the workings of our own company and how our company is stronger and/or weaker than our competition. Remember, knowledge alone isn't enough; it's what we do with it that counts.

8. Master communication techniques, especially listening and nonverbal communication. Most folks are so excited about talking that they don't realize that interested folks usually are more successful than those who are interesting.

9. Networking. Networking is defined as getting together to get ahead. Networking is the way we create visibility, credibility and ultimately greater profitability.

10. Make adversity an adventure. Instead of looking at your glass as half empty, think of it as half full. When something adverse happens be prepared and use the event as a learning experience. The most successful folks I know are the ones who have overcome great adversity.

Part IV:

Sales & Marketing

"You can have everything in life you want, if you will just help other people get what they want."

— Zig Ziglar

Understanding the Relationship Between Marketing and Sales

(Voss)

There is much confusion about the difference between marketing and sales. In a nutshell, marketing looks at the whole business while sales focuses on making a transaction. The two are interdependent. To have a healthy business you need to have both marketing and sales. As BIC Alliance CEO and Founder Earl Heard says in his Alligator Management & Marketing seminars, marketing is stepping up to bat and sales is hitting the ball. The more they interact the better. When sales and marketing are at odds, everyone loses.

The chicken or the egg

So which comes first — marketing or sales? In my view you cannot have one without the other. Marketing can't survive without sales and vice versa. You can have a lot of sales but if the product is not priced profitably, the whole effort is for naught. Part of the marketing effort is to price products competitively and

> *" Marketing is more research, strategic planning and soul searching while sales is more sole on the pavement. "*

profitably. Marketing is more research, strategic planning and soul searching while sales is more sole on the pavement.

Marketing uses research and competitive analysis as well as strategic and tactical planning to maximize market share and plan for growth. Let's say I have a great product that everyone within a square block neighborhood really needs. Marketing has identified this neighborhood. Marketing's cohorts, advertising and public relations, make the neighborhood aware that they have a need and tell them how the great gizmo will answer this need at an affordable price.

Now the salespeople go door to door to sell the great gizmo. After the sales team has done its job, where do we go next? Marketing already has done research that tells us that not all neighborhoods need a great gizmo so we don't waste our time trying to sell where our product is not needed. Armed with a super success story we're off to let advertising, public relations and sales do their thing in another targeted neighborhood where we will repeat our process.

But wait, marketing says there may be some way to goose up the great gizmo so that it does even more for our happy buyers. We can now go back to neighbor-

135

hood one and sell our upgrade. The second sell is easier and more cost effective because we're known throughout the neighborhood (we're branded). The great gizmo did what we said it would do. We've built trust so it takes fewer advertising dollars and practically no in-person sales calls to sell the upgrade. (Remember that in the old days, cameras were practically free because the profit was in the film and film processing. The camera was a once in a decade purchase but the film had to be purchased again and again as did the processing.) In our case the majority of our time and resources can focus on the newly targeted neighborhoods while the upgrade is left to practically sell itself.

The W's and the H

There is a journalistic edict that says every story must answer *who, why, what, where, when* and *how*. Your marketing plan must also answer the *who, what* and *how* of both sales and marketing. The plan defines the ideal customer so you can put these people in the bull's eye of your target market. Your plan also will define exactly what messages will be used to assist initial sales and attract repeat business. It is in this part of your plan that can define the relations you want to build and the reputation you want to create and implement through customer service and follow-up.

The *how* portion of your marketing plan includes advertising, public relations and sales. Each should be defined and communicated openly and effectively within the marketing spectrum so that the plan can be tweaked as customer input is received and market conditions change. Your sales team is key because of their daily personal interaction in the marketplace.

Marketing devises ways to find and educate potential buyers, then lure them to the product and retain them through advertising, public relations, branding, product delivery, customer service and the like. The sales team typically focuses on a one-on-one basis with the end purpose of closing the deal. Good marketing facilitates more and better sales.

Nobody Ever Listened Themselves Out of a Sale

(Phillips)

In my youth, I was told many times that one day I would be a great salesman because I had the "gift of gab." This became a real problem for me until it finally sank in that the most successful sales professionals I knew actually listened more than they talked.

The legendary Ben Feldman, the first insurance salesman to pass the goal of $25 million in one year, when asked his secret to success would always reply, *"Work hard. Think big. Listen well."*

Every major study done in the past 20 years confirms that salespeople need to talk less and listen more. The research shows that sales careers depend upon improved listening. When we listen, we show the customer that we are truly interested in his needs. If we listen well, we will understand those needs and we get the solution right the first time. A good listener will beat a fast talker every time.

" Research shows that sales careers depend upon improved listening."

Unfortunately, we are poorly trained in the skills of listening. In fact, the first sales training many of us got was learning how to give a scripted "presentation" or pitch. This type of training left little or no room for listening at all and generally leads to customer alienation. Typically, the type of orders one would get might be, *"Get out and stay out."* Today there is even less tolerance for this type of approach.

Poor listening is more than just socially unacceptable, it is career inhibiting. The real sales professional must learn to listen well if he is to expect any type of success in the marketplace of today. It would be wise to remember that while many have talked themselves out of a sale, few have listened themselves out of a sale.

Here are some listening principles you can take to the bank:

1. Prepare to listen. The customer holds all of the information we will need to know if we are to answer his needs. We must understand that we can't learn anything new while we are talking. If you are to discover anything about the prospect, you must be prepared mentally to be open to the customer's comments. Since all customers see their needs as unique, it is absolutely critical that we sell

137

him the way he is comfortable buying instead of trying to sell him the way we are comfortable selling.

2. Develop questions that stimulate listening. You and I must develop a list of "open-ended" questions that will get the prospect talking and us listening. "Open-ended" questions are those questions that stimulate conversations beyond one or two word responses like "yes" or "no." Generally an "open-ended" question will start with words like "what," "tell me about," "how," "why," etc. Questions like *"What do you like about your present vendor?"* or *"Why is that important to you?"* will get the prospect giving you valuable information if you are listening.

3. Look for opportunities to listen. There are a lot of salespeople around who think they should be talking when the customer isn't. Many times, however, the prospect may pause to think of a particular point, and that thought can be interrupted by a salesperson. Look for ways to encourage the prospect to talk. Try phrases like: *"Go on." "Tell me more." "I see." "Then what happens?"* These conversation extenders will show the prospect that you are listening and will give him the opportunity to talk about his needs in more depth.

4. Practice the art of listening. Like any skill you want to improve, you will need to practice listening and paying attention to the prospect. I recommend that you consciously practice in conversations outside of the selling situation. Find a selling partner — a sales associate who wants to increase his selling skills — and work on techniques over lunch or early breakfast meetings. Try to keep conversations going by asking open-ended questions that lead the other person to do 80 percent of the talking. (The most natural place to practice is with your family. They will love you for it.) Within a couple of days you will be comfortable enough with this new habit you will want to do it with all of your prospects and customers. They will love it, too.

5. Concentrate on the prospect. Many of us say that we can't remember names, when in fact we just don't pay attention to people. If you will concentrate on listening, you will do a much better job of remembering names. Most selling amateurs are so busy concentrating on what they are going to say next, it's amazing they hear anything. These salespeople want to impress a prospect immediately with either himself or some benefit of whatever they sell. They tell me that the logic of this approach is that they will only have a few minutes with the prospect and want to make an immediate impact. I explain that the prospect is more interested in how much you care about him and his needs than how much you know. If you want to impress a prospect, listen to him and show him that you are more interested in opening a business relationship than *"closing a deal."*

6. Give them feedback. Concentrate on listening with your mind and body as well as your ears. Be an active listener. Make eye contact and show them with your facial expressions and physical manner that you are listening. When you do this, your whole body language will reassure prospects that you are interested in their needs and concerns. The prospect may easily interpret passive listening as indifference. The more feedback they see, the more information they will share with us, better equipping us to find solutions to their situation.

7. Block out distractions. I remember meeting a prospect at a hotel swimming

pool one time. After getting the business he told me that I was the only person he talked to who paid more attention to him than to the women at the pool. I confessed that I wasn't sure which lady might be his spouse, so I didn't dare let my mind wander. A client of mine has a very plush office with a breathtaking view of a beautiful lake surrounded by mountains. It is where he works every day and now, after several years, he takes it for granted. Visitors, however, are constantly distracted by the view. He figures it costs him over a hundred hours a year, just trying to keep people on track. Wherever you are meeting the prospect, you can't afford to let yourself become distracted and waste everyone's time and your attention.

8. Focus on feelings and ideas as much as facts. We need to get factual information like sizes, quantity power requirements etc. but we also need to understand the "why" behind all of the facts. Listening for "feelings" means that we are interested in the intent of the speakers' comments as much as the words. If a prospect says something like, "I think we need to replace our existing system," many salespeople will jump in with a series of features and benefits. On the other hand, a real pro will ask the prospect to explain, *"Why do you feel that way?"* or *"What would you like to accomplish with a new system?"* We need to encourage people to talk about their feelings and ideas and when we do, they will appreciate our concern and help us sell to them.

9. Practice listening with empathy. Most people will not reorder from a company in which the salespeople are indifferent toward their needs. While you may not be indifferent to the needs of your customers, if they think you are, the results will be the same. You and I have to establish empathy or an understanding of our prospect's feelings. Always try to discover something new about your clients and prospects. As you listen to them, try to put yourself in the same situation that they are describing. Once you practice listening with empathy you will begin to see how shallow your listening habits in the past have been.

10. Get confirmation that you heard and understood correctly. You have probably been in situations where two people listen to the same conversation and each walks away with a different message. Make sure you understand what the prospect is saying by asking confirming questions, such as *"To insure that I understand your concerns let me review ... "* When you are able to do this, you will also reassure the prospect that you have listened well. Another benefit is that if you have missed the intent of his comments, they will correct you immediately, which can save you lots of time and lots of lost sales.

Nonverbal, Verbal Communication Skills Equally Important

(Heard)

To most of us, when we think of being an effective communicator, our first thought is our skills at verbal communication. While communicating verbally is important, those skills play only a small part in our overall ability to communicate.

In order for us to excel in communication, we must hone our nonverbal communication abilities, as well as our verbal ones. We must master the skills of listening, body language and effective writing.

Stacey Kidder, a professional counselor and instructor at Louisiana State University, once told a single-parent ministerial training group of which I was a part that almost 90 percent of our communication is nonverbal. As she spoke, I was reminded of the time I devote to teaching listening and other nonverbal skills in my Alligator Management and Marketing seminar. Allow me to share some of Stacey's communication tips.

" Studies show that seven out of 10 waking minutes are spent communicating in some way."

First of all, let's discuss what communication actually is. Communication is the process of sending and receiving information in order to achieve a goal. Communication is how we share facts, feelings, ideas and attitudes. Whatever the purpose, every communication must contain three basic elements. First is the sender who conveys the message. Second is the message itself. Third is the receiver for whom the message is intended.

Studies show that seven out of 10 waking minutes are spent communicating in some way. It may be reading, writing, talking, listening to others or sending nonverbal messages with our body language.

Just think about why good communication skills are important. You may, in fact, want to compile a list, as I did. On my list, I have written that good communication enables us to live a longer, happier, more productive life. For example, where would we be without health-related information? In our personal lives, it helps us to know the best places to live, eat and travel, plus how to get along better with family, friends and associates.

At work, our communication enables us to perform our tasks safely, correctly and profitably. Good communication also enables us to stay motivated and

141

to help motivate others. Whether we are the owner, the president, a supervisor or an employee of a company, how we communicate affects how our workers feel and perform on the job. Good communication helps us encourage, reassure and motivate one another and feel that we and our peers are an important part of the group.

Equally important, communication is the cornerstone of a strong marketing and sales effort. It is critical that our customers, investors, regulatory agencies and the community have confidence in both us and our companies.

The Importance of Continued Learning and the LISTEN Model

(Heard)

In the business world, failure to grasp the intricacies of marketing and sales professionalism can mean the death of your opportunities for success, fame and fortune. It may cause you lifelong financial problems and the loss of respect from your family, friends and business associates. Worst of all, it may even result in a low sense of self worth.

The techniques and nuances of industrial marketing and sales are many and varied. Therefore, mastery of these arts does not come overnight. Rather, it is a process requiring a lifetime of learning. The manifold lessons involved are found not only in books and seminars, but are the result of extensive interaction with seasoned industry professionals who are willing to share their experiences. Regardless of your age, it is never too late to glean expertise, so long as you are willing to invest the time and energy necessary to achieve success.

I am a firm believer in the importance of continued learning. It has always been my belief that a salesperson should expand his knowledge beyond formal education and training, whether he is a beginner or a seasoned veteran.

" Interrupting is often a major mistake salespeople make when trying to push a sale."

Prospecting is the first step toward effective industrial marketing. I suggest that salespeople take what I call the "10 x 10 x 6" approach when developing a database of prospects. Using this approach, the salesperson should outline his top 10 prospects in 10 different industries, along with six contacts per company. In addition, using what I call the "3 x 3 x 3" approach, a salesperson should determine his three primary products or services, the three best reasons why another company should use those products or services, and the three best examples of a client using that product or service in a beneficial way.

With regard to making a sales presentation, communication is of paramount importance. I use the acronym "LISTEN" (Look, Interpret, Stay alert, Think, Encourage and Never interrupt) to illustrate how a typical sales call should be conducted.

Following are the key points of the LISTEN model:

Look: Always show interest in what someone is saying as they speak.

Interpret: Use common sense to make the most of sales opportunities, and interpret what the company will be looking for and what will best help that company's bottom line.

Stay alert: Take notes, ask questions, give prospects choices and stay actively involved in the conversation. The mind works seven times faster when we're listening than when we're speaking, so stay focused.

Think: In discussing business with a potential client, the salesperson should possess the ability to think three-dimensionally, understanding the needs and objectives of both himself and the buyer through third-person analysis. This allows the salesperson to better assess the situation, whether the buyer is eager or unwilling to make a deal. There is no better way to do this than to think like the buyer.

Encourage: Encourage buyers to give more information about their companies. The more that is known about a company, the better the seller is able to establish a relationship and meet the needs of the customer.

Never interrupt: Interrupting is often a major mistake salespeople make when trying to push a sale. Instead, the salesperson should listen carefully to the concerns of the potential buyer and absorb the reasons why he is reluctant to accept a deal, if that is the case. The salesperson should then address the concerns one by one and counteract each reason with solid information designed to change his mind.

In order to effectively communicate benefits of a product or service, the salesperson should also know very well the product, the industry and the competition. Salespeople should also project what I call an "inner smile," an aura of positivity guaranteed to build the prospective buyer's trust in the seller's product or service and make a potential partnership more inviting.

Closing a deal is an end that is equally important to the means. When closing a deal, the salesperson should always establish with the buyer what the next step will be.

Many Companies Grew During the Great Depression

(Voss)

During the 1930s depression many companies actually gained market share. Who were they and how did they do it?

Times were dire. The 1929 stock market collapse saw investors lose a huge percentage of their portfolios. The crash was a leading indicator of a much wider and deeper problem.

Businesses began to close and food prices plummeted so that, in no time, farm income had been cut in half. In 1932 nearly one of every four workers had lost his job. A severe drought swept across the southern plains creating a "dust bowl" as was strikingly described in the John Steinbeck book *The Grapes of Wrath* and portrayed so poignantly in the movie version.

Unemployed workers, and even some families, began to wander across the nation searching for jobs, food and clothing, yet many companies and industries were about to experience a period of growth and increasing market share.

" During a recession and even a depression, businesses that succeed don't let advertising fall into the cracks."

Sticking to it

The 3M Co. didn't quit advertising nor did they cut back on research and development. In 1929, 3M's Dick Drew acted upon a customer's request. The customer was providing insulation for refrigerated railroad cars but their insulation needed a waterproof covering. He sought to wrap the insulation in adhesive-coated cellophane. That didn't solve the customer's problem but it was a first step in the development of Scotch™ Transparent (cellophane) Tape that was introduced in 1930.

In 1935, an Arkansas trucker kept his family fed by hauling produce from Arkansas then selling it for a profit in Chicago. He realized that his truck was sitting idle five months of the year. He thought, why not haul chickens during the nongrowing season? John Tyson's idea was a profitable one. Today the Tyson Co. is a $24 billion business.

GM outpaced Ford

While we're hearing a lot about General Motors™ (GM) and Ford™ these days, in the 1920s Ford outsold GM's Chevrolet by 10 to one. So GM increased

145

its advertising. The company steadily gained market share for its Chevy and when 1931 rolled in they were outselling Ford consistently.

Chevrolet also took advantage of a fledgling new advertising media — the radio. Additionally, the company increased its print advertising. By one account, it was Chevy's ads, along with a couple of other major advertisers, that kept some magazines in business. Next, Chevrolet increased its billboard campaign. After all, if you're driving you're looking at billboards. Perhaps what you're driving isn't what you would like to drive. And that idea was what helped contribute to Chevy's success.

Chevrolet focused on price and quality with an appeal to the emotional side of car buying. One 1930s Chevy ad said, "The new Chevrolet Six is a car of such evident character and quality that it finds a natural place in the most distinguished environment."

Riding the radio waves

Proctor and Gamble™ (P&G) never has walked away from a marketing battle. It is P&G's philosophy that you don't cut advertising during a recession. During the depression the company increased its advertising and began sponsoring many radio shows. Similar to the emotional appeal that Chevrolet went for, P&G sponsored a new type of programming rather than the typical "infomercial." Knowing its audience well, the company created continuing dramas that are still around today and we still call them "soap operas."

Clarence Birdseye introduced the first frozen foods in 1930. Ice cream-maker Howard Johnson expanded his ice cream business into attractive and clean roadside restaurants (and later combo restaurant/motels). The commercial airline business was steadily growing. And movies were becoming a more colorful escape from the problems at hand (in 1930 a number of all-talking, full-color "Technicolor™" features were released). Air travel and entertainment both really took off during the depression years and grew steadily for decades to come.

During a recession and even a depression, businesses that succeed don't let advertising fall into the cracks, they step up their advertising and get more creative with it. They introduce new products that fit the mood or needs of the times. They promote those products/services with all the gusto they've got while their competitors sit and wring their hands. During this recession why don't you advertise with gusto?

Business-to-Business Advertising Yields Results

(Heard)

With the advent of radio, television and online advertising, the perceived value of print advertising has diminished tremendously throughout the years. Many company decision makers are skeptical about investing their advertising dollars into print venues. The benefits of advertising are considered to be somewhat intangible. However, many researchers have concluded that business-to-business advertising can be a very effective tool for not only getting a company message directly to its target market, but for reaching markets that might otherwise have been overlooked.

THE STEPS TO EFFECTIVE MARKETING

There are seven steps that are universally accepted as marketing guidelines and followed religiously by sales executives. Advertising plays a serious role in all of these steps, which include:

• Prospecting. Establishing contact with a prospective customer involves more than simply picking up a telephone. It involves knowledge about the company that you wish to do business with, the services for which they might be looking, what their spending capability is, when money within their budget will be available for expenditures and how best to reach that company. Many times, a phone call by itself is not sufficient to generate interest. Many executives want something tangible that they can study to determine interest in a product or service. Attractive brochures, articles written about your company and product listings provide information not as easily obtainable through a telephone conversation.

• Creating product/service awareness. The key to creating product/service awareness is visibility. The more familiar a prospective customer becomes with a product or service, the more likely they are to make a purchase. Familiarity does not breed contempt in the business world. Conversely, familiarity with a product or service builds trust.

• Garnering interest. The best way in which to create interest in a product or service is to package the product in a professional and attractive manner. Appearance is everything, and the more attractive the product or service is to the customer, the better the chances for a sale become.

" The key to creating product/service awareness is visibility."

• Establishing preference. By legitimately showing how your product or service is superior to those offered by your competitor, you can establish a preference for your services that can become the basis for the future sales. By contrasting your product to others, the customer is given the opportunity to choose, and is more comfortable knowing that product is indeed superior.

• Making effective proposals. An effective proposal is the difference between a yes and a no. State objectives clearly. Describe as much about the product or service as space allows, but be concise. Display price lists and any discounts that may be available. Make the proposal as simple to understand as possible such that the prospective customer does not have to wade through mounds of complicated material.

• Closing the sale. There are several options available when attempting to close a sale. Some companies use pressure tactics, but these should generally be avoided. It is better to offer the prospect a choice between two proposals, always assuming that one will be agreed upon. Go into each closing with the idea that the prospect will say yes. Then make sure that the client understands clearly what has been purchased and that all contracts are signed.

• Ensuring customer satisfaction. After the closing, make sure that the customer is always satisfied with your products and services. Live up to your advertising. When problems arise, address them in a timely manner and do everything in your power to bring about an equitable solution for your customer.

It is obvious that business-to-business advertising plays a vital role in each of these steps, as the more information a prospective client has about your company, the easier the decision to purchase your products and services will become. Print advertising between businesses is indeed a powerful tool to utilize in marketing efforts.

The Importance of Outside-the-Box Thinking

(Heard)

More than 106 million people worldwide watched Super Bowl XLIV, in which the New Orleans Saints defeated the Indianapolis Colts 31-17. Not only did our beloved Saints win their first Super Bowl, they also inspired folks worldwide to believe that adversity can be overcome through hard work, faith and perseverance.

The Saints also proved that in order to be the best, we must think outside the box. When Saints head coach Sean Payton made the decision to call an onside kick at the start of the second half, he shocked not only the Colts but also every spectator in Miami's Sun Life Stadium (I know because my wife Bodi and I, along with our friends and fellow BICsters Ken and Lynette Markle, attended the game) and everyone watching the game on TV. This bold move turned the tide of victory toward the Saints.

A few things came to mind as soon as the Saints recovered that onside kick and engineered the scoring drive that put them in the lead. The first was the old adage "No guts, no glory." The second was how important outside-the-box thinking and action is to achieving success not only in sports but also on the playing field of life.

Just as Saints owner Tom Benson, the coaching staff, the team and the millions of fans that make up the "Who Dat Nation" depended on Coach Payton to make winning decisions, each of us must be willing to think outside the box if we want to succeed in the game of life. Thinking outside the box takes creativity and requires that we keep our cool when others are losing theirs. It means being able to take a calculated risk and having confidence in the team around us to execute the game plan we've so boldly embarked upon.

In good times and bad, marketing our companies and managing our teams also requires outside-the-box thinking and action if we want to have winning organizations. We must think of creative ways for our marketing messages to reach our best clients and prospects not only in the United States but globally as well. This means partnering with the best marketing companies that serve the businesses and/or industries we want to reach.

BIC Alliance, for example, took out an ad in the Super Bowl Sunday edition of the *Miami Herald*. This investment was well worth a chance to inspire readers of the *Miami Herald* to read *BIC Magazine* and learn more about our marketing partners and IVS Investment Banking and BIC Recruiting. Why, you ask, would someone from the business and industrial sector advertise during the Super Bowl? First of all, advertising in a place where the world champion of football is crowned draws corporate executives and decision makers from around the world. Sitting next to Bodi and I were two executives from a power company in Canada, and to the right of us was an executive from the industrial sector in South Louisiana. Second, we wanted to not only help promote our industry and the marketing partners we represent but also to let everyone in attendance know that *BIC Magazine*, a Gulf Coast-based publication, reaches a worldwide audience. (We also bonus distributed *BIC Magazine* in Miami, just as we do at more than 40 other events where business and industry executives from around the world gather each year.)

Now let's think of your business. Whether you own and/or manage a business or an industrial company that reaches a worldwide audience or a local beauty shop or restaurant, there are some places that are better than others for investing your advertising dollars. Note that I used the term "investing" rather than "spending." If you place your advertising in the right spot, it's an investment, but if you place it in the wrong spot, that's a cost. It's also important to remember that advertising doesn't necessarily make your phone ring off the wall. As a matter of fact, most of the time your phone doesn't ring at all. What advertising does is

> " *If you place your advertising in the right spot, it's an investment, but if you place it in the wrong spot, that's a cost.* "

create top-of-mind awareness for your company so that the audience will think of you first when they are in need of a product or service you provide. It also helps buyers know more about your company before they even call. For more than 25 years, several hundred companies have made *BIC Magazine* their publication of choice for reaching executives and decision makers in multiple industries and with various job titles each year.

Another excellent example of outside-the-box thinking took place several years ago when Coach Payton and the Saints management decided to try to build a championship organization around players who were either undrafted — such as running back Pierre Thomas, who shined in the Super Bowl — or were acquired from other teams, like Super Bowl MVP Drew Brees (San Diego Chargers), tight end Jeremy Shockey (New York Giants) and linebacker Jonathan Vilma (New York Jets). Where other coaches and general managers saw limited potential in these men, the Saints saw just the opposite. Can you imagine how Chargers, Giants and Jets fans must feel about their teams' decisions to release these impact players?

Even though a heart surgeon is skilled at performing cardiac surgery, it doesn't mean he can perform a facelift or cure someone whose heart is figuratively broken. In business, we must choose marketing partners that help us put our best face forward and touch the hearts and minds of potential clients. As far as management and marketing are concerned, it takes partnering with other experts, no matter how experienced we are ourselves. Here at BIC Alliance, we don't just depend on our 40-plus years of management experience or our 25-plus years of marketing experience, we also believe in recruiting the best players in Web development, event planning, investment banking and executive recruiting to be part of the BIC Alliance nation. Like the Saints, we are only as strong as our weakest link.

One last thought about outside-the-box marketing is the importance of diversification and utilizing the element of surprise. Just as we wouldn't dream of fishing in only one spot or giving preference to one of our clients over another, we must always be looking for creative ways outside advertising to build top-of-mind awareness of our companies. Being a winner also means helping our communities. The Saints are not only the champions of the NFL, they are also champions at helping rebuild New Orleans, the state of Louisiana and the entire Gulf Coast.

We at BIC Alliance, along with our marketing partners and *BIC Magazine* readers, share many of the same values that made the Saints world champs. The concept of "givers get" has proved itself once again, as the Saints reached the top by giving players from other teams second chances and rookies and undrafted players first chances when they needed them most. Whenever good prevails, "saints" will always be winners — on the field and off. We've found that the secret to our business success and to making *BIC Magazine* the largest multi-industry, multidepartmental energy publication in the Western Hemisphere is to be the best at what we do and practice the notion of "givers get." The concepts of making others No. 1 and thinking outside the box are two of the best marketing tips I know.

Strategies for Before, During, After Trade Show Key to Success

(Heard)

Trade shows are a great way to generate business. By purchasing booth space, one has, in essence, purchased a small business, a meeting place where potential customers can learn of products and services in a setting that is conducive to sales. Trade shows offer an excellent opportunity to interact one on one with potential clients, re-establish business relationships and make invaluable contacts.

Planning is the key to trade show success
Trade shows allow buyers to reduce purchasing costs and confusion, as well as the time it takes to locate suppliers. Exhibitors will want to simplify this process by being prepared, and preparation requires planning.

The first step in planning is research:
• Gather as much information as possible about trade shows from trade publi-

" Networking is one of the most important functions in which companies should participate at trade shows."

cations, journals, directories, colleagues in the industry and associations, among other sources. Determine if it is cost-effective to purchase a booth or if it would be wiser to simply walk the show, make contacts and attend hospitality functions. The key is to pick the right trade show.

• Ask for a list of attendees. Knowing in advance which companies will attend specific shows is invaluable in targeting the market. Presentations can be geared to specific companies as well.

• Ask about registration deadlines. It is important to register early to obtain the best available booth positions to ensure as much pre-show media exposure as possible in the form of news releases, program guides and articles about the show in trade publications.

To ensure that trade show participation is successful, it is important to set goals:

• Create a mission statement that details goals for the trade show. Overall goals should be clarified and exhibits should be shaped to reflect the needs of the

153

customer.

• Determine specific objectives. Objectives keep the focus clear and help team members determine which course of action should be taken. Setting objectives helps measure accomplishments.

• Determine the target audience. It is important to know the audience to specifically gear presentations and exhibited products to the companies that will be most interested. Existing customers, potential customers and unidentified prospects should be targeted in the exhibit.

• Create a plan for promotions. The plan should include who, what, when, where, why and how. Decide which media would be the best to achieve set goals. Set priorities and be conscious of deadlines. Advertising in publications that reach the audience at the show is very important. Be sure to add your booth number to any advertising.

Reasons for participating in trade shows

There are many reasons why a company should participate in trade shows. Aside from the obvious — the generation of revenue — having the opportunity to interface one on one with existing clients is a substantial reason on its own. Other reasons include:

• The opportunity to display new products and services.
• Face to face interaction with prospective buyers.
• Target special interests.
• Reduce time spent on the buying process.
• Qualify new buyers.
• Gain product and service feedback.
• Recruit new personnel.
• Create new customer lists.
• Distribute samples of new products.
• Make new contacts.
• Communicate message to a new market.
• Learn about buying preferences.

Using promotional materials

Promotional materials are an integral part of attracting people to the booth, and preshow promotions should be considered a necessary element of the budget. There are many different ways to promote an exhibit, including invitation letters, brochures, display signs, passes, drawings and giveaways or sponsoring an event.

Networking is invaluable during trade shows

Networking is one of the most important functions in which companies should participate at trade shows. The opportunity for face-to-face interaction with people in the industry who would be otherwise unavailable provides businesses with unlimited potential for additional revenue and growth.

Everywhere one goes at a trade show presents an opportunity to network

— hotel lobbies, restaurants, competitions, workshops, exhibitor booths and hospitality suites. Of these, hospitality suites present the greatest opportunity for contacts to be established.

Be familiar with and prepared to represent the company in a knowledgeable and professional manner. Prepare a list of questions that will trigger more than a yes or no response to establish the willingness of one's company to listen. Host a hospitality event if the company can afford to, but always make sure that representatives from the company are available to answer questions or explain products and services.

Attract prospects to the exhibit booth

The exhibit booth is an excellent tool through which the company can communicate its message. Sales-effective booths have visual impact, are user-friendly and exude an air of comfort. Several helpful hints should be followed in order to realize maximum results from the booth:

• Advertise in trade publications regularly. Be sure to list the booth number, and invite trade show attendees to visit the booth.

• Send invitations to the exhibit early — usually 40 to 60 days in advance.

• E-mail reminders 20 to 40 days in advance.

• Telephone guests seven to 10 days in advance.

• Make sure that graphics are displayed in a way such that the viewer is visually attracted to the booth.

• Use vivid colors, as color attracts attention.

• Do not stack brochures on the table. Display them in a neat and orderly manner.

• Create an area where visitors can browse.

• Do not try to pitch to visitors. The object is to make contacts and familiarize visitors with the company's services.

• Identify what products attract attention.

• Make sure your booth is well-lit at all times.

After-show follow-up is vital

Follow-up after the show is very important. This is what will generate additional revenue for the company, and will be a factor in determining if the exhibit was a worthwhile investment. After-show activities should include:

• Follow up on all leads. Prior to the show, determine how many leads should be obtained and set a specific timeline for the pursuit of those leads.

• Evaluate the show. Understanding performance is the only way to improve upon it. Decide what was effective and what was not. Determine what improvements need to be made.

• Collect business cards. Make sure that employees write notes on the backs of the cards describing the products or services in which that particular person is interested. This will aid in determining if that company is a prospect or should be added to the mailing list.

• Use visitor information wisely. Collect as much visitor information as possible. Move fast, but not too fast. Send "thank you" notes to clients and prospects.

155

Add individuals and companies to the mailing list. Commit to being available when companies are ready to buy products and services.

And remember ...

When planning, participating in or following up on a trade show, it is important to keep in mind:

- Every show is a valuable learning experience.
- Planning is the most important aspect of one's involvement in the show.
- Select the right show.
- Interfacing one on one with clients and prospects is more important than the hard sell.
- Preshow promotions are a must.
- Network. Network. Network.
- Budget wisely.
- Provide training for the exhibit staff.
- Follow up on all leads.
- Use experience to make improvements.

Networking Strategies

(Heard)

Network: a group, system, etc., of interconnected or cooperating individuals.
Networking: the developing of contacts or exchanging of information with others in an informal network, as to further a career.
(Source: Webster's New World College Dictionary; 4th ed.)

One of the most important aspects of marketing a product or service is networking. My definition of networking is getting together to get ahead. In order to successfully utilize the networking process there are many rules to follow regarding who, what, when, where, how and why.

" Networking can be accomplished anytime and anywhere."

Who?

Who will be your target audience? Choose companies or individuals that will not only benefit you from a financial standpoint but also base your decision on reputation, quality, service and compatibility.

Determine how many companies you wish to reach. Set goals that are consistent with your ability to produce. If you overextend yourself by trying to reach too many companies at once, your ability to follow up may be limited. It is better to make solid contacts that produce results with a few companies than to make flimsy contacts with many companies.

What?

What do you hope to accomplish through the use of networking? Establish what image you want to project in the industry, then be able to back that image up.

Determine what products or services are the primary focus of your networking campaign, then stress the good points of those products and services to potential clients.

Decide what makes you different from similar companies offering similar services. Make the most of those differences. Play them up to potential clients.

When?

When is the best time for your company to implement networking procedures? Networking can be accomplished anytime and anywhere. You represent your company no matter where you go or what you do.

Organized networking at trade shows costs money. As soon as your company can comfortably budget participation in trade shows, then networking at these shows should be a priority. Personal contacts generate revenue. Revenue promotes growth.

Where?

Where do I find networking opportunities? Trade journals, newspapers and magazines are excellent sources to discover when and where networking opportunities will be available. News releases are another good source.

Restaurants, golf courses, hotel lobbies and sports events also present good networking opportunities. While you cannot have too many personal contacts, it's usually a good practice to limit your hard-hitting sales pitch to companies that show real interest in what you are selling. However, no matter where you are and who you are talking to, always project the image of your company in a positive manner.

How?

How do I reach these companies? Research plays an important role in reaching potential customers. Business and trade publications and the Internet are excellent tools through which to find out about companies and how to reach them. *BIC Magazine*, for instance, reaches 120,000 key decision makers and is read online in its entirety.

The media provides an abundance of useful information about companies that should be carefully scrutinized for clues as to preferences. Mailing lists are another way to determine which companies you should approach and how you can reach those companies.

Phone calls, e-mail, invitations to company functions and attendance at trade shows are just a few useful tools to attract future business. Hospitality suites are also an excellent source for meeting and attracting new clientele.

Why?

Why should you bother with networking at all? Your company produces a good product. Your service is second to none. Your business will sell itself, right? Wrong.

Networking creates opportunities for sales, growth, future alliances and projects, and keeps your company in the forefront of the latest ideas and technologies. By interacting with other companies in a more relaxed environment, you are not only creating an image for your company, but you are learning about other products and services that can be useful to you at a later date.

Effective networking

The best networkers, like the best communicators, are not those who focus on themselves, but instead concentrate their efforts on filling the needs of others. In essence, this means linking someone with a need with someone who can fulfill that need.

Many opportunities can be found within the networking experience:
• Mutual support between networking members.
• Solid contacts.
• Leads and referrals.
• Showcase products and services.
• Job banks.

Communication in networking

Communication skills are a very important part of networking. Knowing when to approach someone, how to begin and maintain a conversation, and knowing when and how to end a conversation are the keys to becoming an excellent communicator:
• Be the first to say hello.
• Shake hands warmly. Do not exert too much or too little pressure during the handshake.
• Pay attention to the person's name and repeat it.
• Notice small details about the other person and use that as a conversation starter.
• Be sincere. People are quick to recognize insincerity.
• Have questions ready so that the conversation does not stall.
• Keep questions conversational.
• Pay close attention to the enthusiasm with which the other person talks about different topics. This will give you clues about what should be the focus of the conversation.
• Make sure follow-up questions are positive.
• Always close the conversation on a positive note.

159

Networking protocol

Many trade shows and conferences provide hospitality suites, which are a great place to practice networking skills. While many people may view hospitality suites as a place to party, it is important to follow the rules of etiquette when visiting the suites:

• For business after hours, regular business clothes are appropriate, although a little dressier look may be in order.

• Keep body language on the conservative side.

• Limit yourself to two drinks and do not substitute cocktail foods for your supper.

• Avoid messy foods.

• When being introduced or introducing someone, always shake hands.

• Be sure to wear your name tag on the upper right hand side of your garment.

• Smile immediately whenever eye contact is made with anyone.

• Always be professional, and remember — the image you project becomes the image of your company.

Gauging success

Successful networking is accomplished through the building of relationships. Truly caring about others is the secret. Everyone appreciates sincerity, and that is the foundation upon which strong business relationships are formed.

Networking has been successful for you when:

• The relationship established is mutually rewarding; both parties gain something from the relationship, whether it be contacts, profits, contracts, referrals or perhaps simply the relationship itself.

• You have helped someone, or someone has helped you to achieve a measure of success, whether large or small.

• You find that you are giving as much as you are receiving.

• Every introduction is viewed as an opportunity to build a relationship.

• You can see the benefits of the alliances that you have built.

The New Nice

(Phillips)

"I really care about my customers," Terry told me as we ╰.╰.╰ ╰.╰.╰╰╰ ╰╰ an appointment. *"I try to do the very best I can for them and make sure that their needs are met."* *"Sounds good,"* I thought to myself. *"But I wonder if it's true."*

Most sellers I know go to great pains to point out to me just how customer-focused they are. They want to make sure I know that they're not pushy or manipulative or sleazy in any way. Yet, when they get into meetings with prospective clients, they quickly switch into a seller-centric mode of operation before they even know what's happening. That's exactly what occurred in my sales call with Terry. Before we went in, I asked her to tell me what she'd said to get the appointment.

" If you're not listening and totally tuned into what your customer is saying, you're not being nice — you're being rude!"

"I told him that we'd introduced some exciting new products (or services) that I thought could help reduce turnaround time in their production area," Terry told me.

While the meeting appeared to have a customer-centric agenda, what actually played out during our time with the prospect was an entirely different matter.

After a few minutes of genial exchanges and a bit of data gathering about the business and operation, the decision maker asked Terry about her new products.

She started talking about them. She pulled out brochures. She showed samples. And she kept on talking answering his questions, one-by-one, in excruciating detail. (Her product marketing manager would have been proud of all she remembered!)

Before we knew it, her time was up and we were escorted to the lobby. The decision maker thanked us for our time and instructed Terry to keep in touch. Out we walked, empty-handed with no hope of ever selling anything. But Terry was customer-focused, right? She graciously answered all his questions and told him exactly what he wanted to know about her offering.

I'm sorry. I beg to disagree. Terry wasted that man's time. She wasn't one bit concerned about his business operation. She just cared about being perceived as a service-oriented and helpful person.

Your job today is to help customers figure out how to improve their business operations. That means increasing or decreasing something — and especially "something" that's tied in to one of their key business metrics.

Here are several ideas on how you can truly be customer-centric in today's marketplace:

1. Become an expert in your client's business. Nothing beats an immersion course. Roll up your sleeves and become an apprentice for a week. Identify the goals and objectives, mission-critical business imperatives and critical success factors. Find out what's happening in their industry. Learn how your product or service fits into their workflow. Discover where the gaps are — what kind of problems occur in their current process or methodology. Explore the business ramifications of these problems and the value of solving them.

Some sellers tell them they can't take the time to do this, that they need to be out making sales calls and signing contracts. Or they say their boss won't let them do this. Yet, their customer knowledge is so shallow — and I mean incredibly shallow — that they can't even hold an intelligent conversation with a key decision maker for longer than five minutes.

You can't be customer-centric if you don't understand your client's business. You can only show them your offering, albeit in a very nice manner, and hope that they understand the difference it makes in their organization.

2. Avoid early product/service discussions. Many sellers inadvertently set themselves up to talk about their products or services right away. In phone calls to prospective buyers, they mention their new "stuff" to get their foot in the door. With this type of lead-in, they're guaranteed to be asked to talk about their offerings. Requests for appointments should always focus on business results. When asked about your products in a first sales call, answer very briefly and guide the conversation back to the prospect's business. It's not nice to waste your customer's time talking about something that may be entirely irrelevant to their business.

3. Prepare your questions ahead of time. You may not know this, but top sellers always prepare a list of questions to ask before they go on the call. In fact, these questions are carefully planned to elicit very specific types of information about the customer's business, goals, objectives, current situation, challenges and more.

You can't be customer focused unless you write your questions down. Otherwise, when you're talking to a prospective client you'll continually be thinking of what you'll say next. If you're not listening and totally tuned into what your customer is saying, you're not being nice — you're being rude!

Honestly, the real key in selling is to not delude yourself into thinking that being nice is what customers are looking for. They don't need more friends. Nor do they really care about your product/service offering.

Customers want someone to help them improve their business. They want a seller who brings them ideas and insights. That's what's valuable today — it's the new nice.

Note: Asking good questions is the most important sales skill of all when you finally meet with a prospective customer. In addition, research shows that most sellers really miss the boat in terms of what kinds of questions they ask and in what sequence.

162

You Can Dress Her Up, But . . .

(Voss)

There's an old saying, "You can dress her up, but you can't take her out." Yep, it's a sexist remark for sure, but it has the ring of truth. The point of the adage is that you can put the most beautiful designer clothes on a woman (or man), but if they don't have the poise and manners that polite society expects, then even the most lovely façade will be just that — a façade.

The same is true with companies. They can put their best foot forward, but if they don't deliver services to the market's satisfaction, people catch on and think of them as "all fluff and no stuff." I don't see much of this. Most companies survive by delivering a reasonable service or product in a timely manner and thereby creating a sustainable repeat business.

" If your advertising looks outdated and tired, Mr. Investor is probably going to get the idea that your business is also outdated and tired."

Now, let's rephrase that old adage to say, "If your company is good enough to be taken out, why not dress her up so she can get the attention she deserves?" I think this is what I've seen lacking the most during my career in business-to-business advertising/marketing. Many companies have grown to become respected within the industry they serve, but they have never learned the value of marketing. Yet, it is the marketing that will take them to a new level.

Dreams alone don't get you there

If owners dream of going public or if they want to sell the company, it is advance planning and marketing that will prepare them for the transition or the transaction. (Who's going to buy stock in your company or even buy your company if they don't know who you are and what it is that you do and how well and profitably you do it?)

One of my clients made the transition from private to public, but it was a long time coming. First, they really beefed up their public relations and their advertising. Then, they reigned in some of the renegade companies they owned and made sure everyone was on the same page. Next, a cohesive image was created and presented to their customer base and financial markets. During the process, they eliminated a lot of internal "roadblocks" that did not contribute to increased performance or give added value to their services (from their customers' point of view, not their view of what they thought customers wanted).

Long story short, they are now in Warren Buffett's portfolio.

So, you don't know that you don't know?

One of the main problems is that people don't know when to get out of the way. They think because they know their business inside/out and they've been successful to this point that they can do the same as they've always done and go the rest of the way. They don't want professional help (and probably distrust it). They just don't know that they don't know. They don't imagine themselves behind a desk on Wall Street and ask, "What would attract my attention and pique my interest in one company over another?"

Their homemade looking, time-warped brochures with the company logo showing in every photo (the same logo that cousin Dan Draftsman drew up 30 years ago) just doesn't cut it today. The way you go about performing your services may not have changed, but communications has exploded. If your advertising looks outdated and tired, Mr. Investor is probably going to get the idea that your business is also outdated and tired, and he will look to a brighter star or certainly to a more interesting possibility.

Having an attractive, functional and easy-to-navigate Web site is important too. The first thing Mr. Wall Street will do is to check you out on the Web. So, let's say the young slickster lands on your site and sees your "Newsroom" section but what's posted is two or more years old! Good grief! That's not good. So be sure to have a good, well-designed, well-planned Web site that serves customer needs first but also gives a clear overview of your company (a nice Web site can make you look even bigger than you are).

If you're fishing for a buyer, give him some bait — something he can sink his teeth into. For investors, give them a little help with their sales pitch so they can round up fellow investors. They need to be sold on you before they can sell you to others.

Now, go out and put some lipstick and foo-foo powder on your company's face because if you're going to take her out she needs to look like the beauty no one's eyes can resist.

Making An Effective Sales Presentation

(Strickland)

Even the "natural born" salesperson needs to continually hone his presentation skills. Ongoing preparation is key to making an effective sales pitch. The more interesting and compelling the pitch, the more likely a decision will be made in your favor.

One of the first rules is to know as much as you can about your audience. Using the same old canned presentation again and again is a one-size-fits-all approach that is soon delivered by rote and without enthusiasm. Every audience is different and so should every sales pitch be different. The goal is to learn client needs/problems, and then lay out, in a clear and concise way, exactly how your company can and will address those needs and has solved similar problems.

A presentation is as much a "probing" session as it is a sales pitch. A good salesperson listens carefully and responds respectfully and knowledgeably without being braggadocios or a know-it-all.

" One of the first rules is to know as much as you can about your audience."

Who should be on the presentation team?

Because a salesperson does not know it all, it is wise to include a technical person, such as an engineer or project manager, in the presentation. Selling goes against most engineers' instincts, so the salesperson must take the lead then allow the engineer or project manager to step up and address technical issues.

Keep the presentation team to a limited few. To walk in with an army is detrimental to the purpose. Also, remember to keep the tempo upbeat and invigorating. If your audience starts to nod off or begin looking at the clock or at their cell phones, you know you're beginning to lose them, so step up the pace.

Be prepared and rehearse

Make certain that everyone on the team is aware of the objectives. Keep these in mind as you prepare any PowerPoint® charts or other visual aids. Also remember that people learn or absorb information in different ways. Eleven percent of people learn through what they hear and 83 percent learn by what they see. Research further says that people retain about 20 percent of what they hear, 30 percent of what they see and 50 percent of what they both see and hear. So, a good mix of verbal and visual is a good thing.

Retention drops significantly after the first 24 hours, so it is good to have a professionally prepared "leave behind" like a brochure and some of the visuals and key points you made. If the meeting drifted away from what you have in print, then you can always follow up a few days later by sending attendees a reminder of what was discussed and your solutions.

Rehearsing is good. It allows even the savviest salesperson an opportunity to practice their presentation skills and gives the technical guys an opportunity to hone their skills in front of a large group. It also doesn't hurt to use some techniques that professional speakers use. The pros can give you hints on posture, body language, eye contact, voice level and more. You can practice your delivery by speaking into a tape recorder and then playing it back. It's good to know what you sound like when you talk about your company's services.

Also, if possible, learn as much as you can about whom you will be presenting to. Who is the real decision maker? Who is the leader, and who are the followers? Your audience can range from 100-percent purchasing people or planners, or construction managers. It can also consist of a mix of all of these and more. Your meeting needs to appeal to each contingency so use common sense; what would the planner be interested in? What is purchasing interested in?

Everyone on your presentation team needs to be properly attired. Good grooming, pressed clothing and well-shined shoes says you care about your appearance so you will probably also care about their project too. Clothing should be conservative and comfortable.

My dad has always told me that, "Ninety-eight percent of a client's decision-making process is perception." Creating the perception that you are professional, knowledgeable, helpful and interested in helping customers solve their problems goes a long way when you sincerely believe in your company's services.

So, go forth and make your presentation memorable as you differentiate your company from your competition.

The Making of a Salesman

(Strickland)

When I began my career I never dreamed that I would find myself in a sales position. My early aspiration was to become a project manager. But, my wife wanted a lifestyle with a guaranteed income and less travel.

Since I was a craftsman, I knew many others in the field, so I applied for a human resources position with AltairStrickland. You would think that the son of one of the company founders wouldn't have to apply, but that wasn't the case. I, like everyone else, had to prove that I was qualified and could do the job. I finally did get the job. Some of my duties were to contact field crews, making sure they had the skills and current credentials required, and to mobilize them for the upcoming projects. I was on the phone and computer constantly trying to track down the appropriate craftspeople. I was also receiving calls from those looking for work.

> " It is important to bid only on those jobs
> in which your company and the client
> have similar core values. "

Two years later, our top salesman, Ron Thomason, left. I knew Ron well and knew that it would be difficult to fill his shoes. He was an outstanding salesman; sales seemed to come naturally and almost effortless for him. I, on the other hand, am not a born salesman.

Nonetheless, I applied for Ron's position and was granted the title of "salesman" on a tentative basis. I would have to prove to management that I could maintain relationships with existing clients and attract new business. It was a daunting task. While sitting in the human resources chair, I made and received hundreds of calls a day. The silence of the Thomason-vacated sales office was ear shattering. After about a week of quiet I decided to embark on a three-year plan.

Marketing

My first thought was, "Here we are one of the best companies in the business. We're known for our FCCU specialty services in some circles, but not in others. We are doing great work, but few people are aware of the quality and spectrum of services we provide." I needed to get the word out.

I began by taking pictures of our projects and compiling case studies that explained the project scope, complexity and the value that was added via our constructability expertise and our truly outstanding and dedicated craftspeople.

We had performed a complex FCCU revamp for Williams Refinery that was presented at an NPRA conference, still few knew of it. So, I prepared a case study about that project and then featured it in a trade magazine article.

I next consulted an advertising agency about how we could publicize and showcase these achievements on a much broader basis. The agency and I came up with a sensible budget that coincided with my three-year plan.

Asking questions

Another part of my three-year plan was to visit our clients and ask questions rather doing all the talking as some salesmen do. I wanted to ask questions like, "Can you see the value of our company to your organization?" I also asked myself this question, "Is this client a good fit with our procedures and principles?"

I learned that listening is most important. I also learned the value of the follow up. After selling the project, one must get involved. Ask questions of your clients and your own people to see if there is anything that can be fixed before it becomes a problem. After the project, ask what went right and what went wrong. Report these perceptions/remarks to your managers. If your company is attentive, things can markedly improve due to the feedback. (If you receive kudos it makes everyone want to continue to do well; if you receive criticism it points out where improvement is needed.)

Become a source

Another thing I decided to do was to educate myself about the many refinery processes and the intricate details of operations. I also believe that it is important to constantly study the market. I keep informed by reading trade magazines and business publications and am involved in various industry blogs and Internet sites relative to the business we are in. There is a lot of information available about contract issues and other topics that affect contractor/client relationships.

My experience in fieldwork served me well to a point, but after learning and continually studying the many other things about our work, I found that I also could be an information source to the clients. This helps me be of more value to the clients and to our company.

A rifle as opposed to a shotgun

I know salespeople who chase every project in the industry whether or not the company they represent has the expertise required. This shotgun approach tends to waste time and money. It can also clog your estimating department as they prepare bid after bid proposal. I prefer a rifle approach in which you target only those projects that require your company's core competencies. This way your estimating department can do what they do best and not be overwhelmed with hard-to-bid projects or waste valuable time and assets on those least profitable projects.

It is also important to bid only on those jobs in which your company and the client have similar core values. For a project to be successful it helps if everyone's on the same page when it comes to having realistic expectations and mutual understanding.

Organization and consistency

Some of the best salespeople I know are also the most organized and consistent. One man called on me for years before I ever purchased anything from him. He did not make a pest of himself and had respect for the value of my time, but he did stay in touch on a quarterly basis. Meanwhile, I found him to be a valuable source of information. His company had an extensive research department and had gathered industry statistics for years and made annual forecasts about the number of projects, locations and estimated expenditures.

One day I was at a point that what he was selling became a good tool for my marketing plan, and sure enough "steady Eddie" was there. Needless to say, I preferred him to his competitors because of his consistency and helpfulness in the past, and I also was well educated as to the exact value his product would provide.

Energetic strength and good attitude

A good salesperson needs stamina. Thankfully, long lunches with intoxicating drinks are a thing of the past. A good salesperson is alert and at the top of their game. It is important to get plenty of sleep, to exercise and to eat healthfully. When we feel good we naturally do better — our posture is better, our eyes are brighter, and we just make a better impression. I find travel to be a hassle and tiring so I try to schedule appointments after I have had time to rest or freshen up.

Don't discount visualization techniques

When I was a boilermaker I used visualization. Before doing my job I would visualize that I would perform it well and leave the plant safely. I found that it helped me stay focused on the job to become more safety aware. Working in the field cannot only be dangerous, but it is stressful too.

Salespeople experience a different kind of stress. Travel is stressful and rejection is too — there is not a salesperson alive who has not experienced rejection. Visualization techniques can help reduce stress and anxiety.

Many professional athletes and successful business people use visualization. Mental imagery is different than rational or linear thinking as it engages a different part of the mind. It is a powerful mental tool that can actually help you physically too.

Where Fear Ends, Life Begins

(Phillips)

If you have been in sales long enough you have felt the paralyzing grip of fear of rejection or failure. There are few things in a selling career as debilitating as the fear that makes you waste time on less threatening tasks, that keeps you from picking up the telephone or keeps you circling the block instead of parking and making the call.

I can speak from experience. I have been there and fought the battles, won some and lost a lot of them. Early in my selling career, I became an expert at avoiding possible rejection. I could have a plaque on the wall for some of my more creative tactics.

Fear of rejection became an art form for me. I could drive past a prospect's office and determine if it was a good time to make a call. Here's how the system worked: If the parking lot was full, it meant he must have an important meeting going on and would be too busy to see me. If there were empty parking places, it meant he must not be in the office.

With that kind of logic, you could talk your way out of ever being rejected by a customer. You would, however, have to face skinny kids and a short-tempered spouse who doesn't dress very well when you got home every night. Fortunately, for me, my wife enjoys her status in the MasterCard Hall of Fame and I had to either sell or I would find myself on some debtor's island somewhere.

I knew if things didn't change, I would be in deep trouble. Things didn't change and I was soon in deep trouble. That's when I discovered that things wouldn't change until I changed. And when I did change, the results were amazing.

I found, as have many others, that as I faced my fears and overcame them, I felt exhilaration uncommon in my career. It's called living and enjoying life. Let's take a real look at fear of failure.

Failure can be a benefit

Occasional failure can be counted on to keep us on our toes! I can't tell you how many times I have learned this lesson the hard way. (The "hard way" is losing a "sure thing" to a competitor who would never have a chance if you or I were doing our job correctly.)

Failures will keep us hungry and striving to be our best because we realize that sometimes it will take everything we have to get the positive results we want and deserve. You can always trust failure to keep you humble. Failure is a great motivator and learning tool.

Failure is a learning experience

Watch a child learning to walk. My guess is that the baby will fall hundreds

171

of times before its legs are strong enough to take those first few faltering steps. You and I have a lot to learn as well. The trick is to learn from our bruises.

I am going to recommend that you always try to learn from your setbacks. One of the best ways to do this is to ask the prospect. You would be amazed what you will discover if you sincerely ask what you could have done better to help the prospect make a decision to buy from you.

Failure is a numbers game

We have heard it hundreds of times but it is still true. If you fail enough times, the percentages will catch up with you. Years ago I was driving to an appointment with my Xerox mentor, Bob Vining, when he unexpectedly pulled into a parking lot and said, "Follow me. This will only take a minute."

As soon as we got in the door, a gentleman approached us and said, "Vining, why do you keep coming in here? I have told you I don't want to buy a Xerox machine." Bob responded, "I keep coming in here because my boss told me I have to get six people to tell me 'No' before one will buy from me, I just need to

" Failure is a great motivator and learning tool."

get my 'No' quota for the day and I knew I could trust you to help me out."

Bob got a lot of "No's" but he also taught me a lot about sales and, as you've probably guessed, he got the prospect in this example as well.

Destructive

Where failure begins to have its most destructive effect is in the anticipation of failure. The fear we feel is most times unsubstantiated but it often becomes a self-fulfilling prophecy. We hear ourselves say things like, "I just knew I wouldn't get that order" or "I had a bad feeling about this prospect."

Fear makes us waste our potential. If we go into a situation feeling dread, chances are our fears will be fulfilled. We learned this in grade school. If you are like most of us you can remember times when you told a classmate, "I know this test will be a disaster." What happened? If you passed the test, you considered yourself lucky!

So, what's the solution? Actually, there are three areas we can work on.

Mindset

The first thing to do is to get our minds clear of all of the negatives. There is a lot of doubt about the effectiveness of "visualization." I can't tell you what to think about visualization but I can recommend something that works for me. Before picking up the telephone, making a call on a client or stepping on stage before a new audience, I will take a few moments, completely relax and remember (or visualize) a specific time and event when I did everything right.

172

I will recall the preparation, my ability to respond on the spot and come up with just the right answers. I will think of a time when I was cool under pressure, when things just really worked well and people congratulated me afterward. I will visualize some of the customers I have sold and how pleased they were after they had become my customer.

This technique helps put me in a state of mind that is very positive and relaxed. After that, I am prepared to examine my expectations.

Expectation management

Expectation is the difference between success and failure. What do you expect to accomplish when making the next sales call? You can't expect a sale on each call. So what do you expect? This is very important because the difference between failure and success is the difference between what we expect and what we get.

If you go into a "cold call" situation with a plan and expectation to get an appointment and you get it, you have made a successful call. What we encourage our sales winners to do is to break the selling process down into several logical steps. Each sale then would have a number of successful steps. Expectation management is the ability to understand (in numbers) what successes we expect each day.

How do you set these expectations? If the problem is that you are not making any "new business" calls, then perhaps an expectation of 20 new business calls per day is too threatening. Let's decide that I can make one per hour, between existing customer calls. Once you are comfortable with that, we can stretch it to two per hour and so on. You will find that once you begin your plan your fears will drift away.

The key is to set up a plan and then work the plan. Understand where you need and want to be and then put numbers to the plan and make it work for you.

If Jesus, Moses, Mohammed and Buddha couldn't sell 100 percent of their prospects, who are you to think you can?

Risk management

Risks are those events that make us step out of our comfort zone. Each time we take a risk we learn and we stretch ... we grow. Implicit in the word "risk" is the word "reward." We can earn something for each risk we take. I encourage my sales professionals to put risk in a whole new perspective, one where we will either get a reward or we will learn something. That is all there is to the risk.

If you get turned down, you are no worse off than if you had not asked for the sale at all. At least if we ask and are turned down, we are in a position to learn something. If we never take the risk and ask for the order (or even the appointment), we can never take another risk and ask why we have been turned down.

Find 'life' in courage

If we allow ourselves to settle for less than our best, we are giving up a portion of our character and that will affect our self-esteem. You are not alone in your call reluctance. We have all been there and it takes a great deal of courage to put it behind you. And if you are like me, it will never disappear completely. Aleksandr Solzhenitsyn said it very clearly, " ... from ancient times a decline in courage has been considered the first symptom of the end." Don't let fear of failure have its way with you. Life is too short to live in fear.

Selling Our Ideas to Others

(Heard)

Success in our personal lives and business lives goes hand in hand. Have you ever wanted something so badly that you blundered while trying to sell your idea to the person or people who ultimately decided whether or not to help fulfill your desire and buy your product or idea?

First of all, it's important to remember that timing is everything. Even the best idea or product in the world can be rejected if it is presented at the wrong time. Recently my wife Bodi and I, along with our partners, Thomas and Dane Brinsko, planned to attend an LSU football game. We checked the weather report in the hours before kickoff — on that particular day, the likelihood of a thunderstorm was 90 percent. It was drizzling when we left our home.

Earlier in the day, knowing that the weather was going to be miserable, Thomas and I went to a store that sold LSU merchandise and stood in line with dozens of others who were buying rainwear. When the rains came during the game, we stayed dry while thousands of other spectators got drenched.

> **" 'No' doesn't necessarily mean 'no' forever, it simply means 'no' for now."**

Timing and circumstances always play an important part in what, when and where we buy and must always be considered in what, when and where to sell.

We've always heard that the squeaky wheel gets the grease. While we may think that our idea or product is the most important thing our bosses or our buyers should have on their "things to do list," the simple truth is that the priorities of others are rarely the same as our own. We've got to be able to put ourselves in the other person's shoes, whether you're a child dealing with a parent, a husband or wife selling an idea to a spouse, an employee selling an idea to a boss or owners or a salesman presenting a product or service to an existing client or prospect.

Here are a few ideas that you may want to think through very carefully when selling an idea, a product or a service.

• We never get a second chance to make a first impression.

• Manners matter in every presentation, especially in handling rejection. Losing our cool when we're rejected is the best way I know of to lose future opportunities to have our ideas and products selected. "No" doesn't necessarily mean "no" forever, it simply means "no" for now. So when we get a "no", we need to patiently try to find the best time and circumstances to present our idea

175

or product again.

• It's important that we know how to state our ideas clearly, whether they're spoken, written or expressed through other forms of nonverbal communication. It's also important to present the idea and proposal in such a manner that the person you're making your presentation to can easily explain to others your idea and/or product. So spend time preparing and practicing your presentation regardless of how large or small the opportunity might be. Building small relationships today can open big doors later and perhaps even bigger referrals immediately.

• Explain and show why your idea and/or product should be of value to the other person or organization.

• Share both the pros and the cons of the product or idea and address any objections as part of the presentation so it doesn't become an issue later on. It's been said that we should think of objections like weeds in a garden and pull them out regularly before they ruin the crops.

• Last but not least, offer several different options instead of seeking a yes-or-no response. I always approach a presentation as though I'm selling a Ford Motor Co. car or product. I offer the Lincoln, the Mercury and the Ford and explain that each option will get the driver where they want to go. The ultimate choice is just a matter of style, how they'd like to travel, the perception they'd like to create and the best investment at that particular time.

Compromise is the key component in selling an idea, whether it's at home or at work. If everyone isn't happy, no one is happy in the long run. Therefore, it is important to remember that our key long-term relationships are far more important than one-time sales. Furthermore, partial acceptance is better than no acceptance at all.

Part V:

Wisdom of the Ages

"Blessed is the man who finds wisdom, the man who gains understanding, for he is more profitable than silver and yields better return than gold."

— Proverbs 3:13-14

Wisdom in Quotes

Below are some of our favorite quotes and nuggets of wisdom, all of which remain powerful and poignant to this day despite the fact that some were first scrawled or uttered ages ago.

1. Today is the first day of the rest of our lives.

2. Learn more, earn more.

3. Show me someone who is afraid of losing his job, and I'll show you someone who likely will.

4. You can't lose business you don't have, so don't be afraid to go for it.

5. We are full of weaknesses and errors; let us mutually pardon each other for our follies. (Voltaire)

6. Some people would rather climb a tree to tell a lie than stand on the ground and tell the truth.

7. The better you listen, the more you will glisten.

8. It's better to be perceived as a fool than to open your mouth and leave no doubt.

9. God gave us two ears and one mouth so that we'll listen twice as much as we talk.

10. A bird in the hand is better than two in the bush.

11. Don't bite off more than you can chew.

12. Take the low hanging fruit first.

13. Don't go after a territory you can't take and don't take a territory you can't hold.

14. Think before you speak.

15. A bad workman always blames his tools.

16. A penny saved is a penny earned.

17. If you make others No. 1, they'll realize how brilliant you are and respond in kind.

18. Givers get.

19. Networking is defined as getting together to get ahead.

20. A stitch in time saves nine.

21. It's hard to be a prophet in your own domain.

22. Every dog has its day.

23. The harder we work, the luckier we are.

24. Never cry over spilled milk.

25. If at first you don't succeed, try, try again.

26. Time is a great healer.

27. The early bird gets the worm.

28. You never get a second chance to make a first impression.

29. An ounce of prevention is better than a pound of cure.

30. Stop and smell the roses.

31. Every rose has a thorn.

32. Better late than never.

33. If you can't say something nice, don't say anything at all.

34. There is no big "I" or little "u" in "team."

35. A rolling stone gathers no moss.

36. Father Time waits for no one.

37. The older we get, the wiser we are.

38. Birds of a feather flock together.

39. You can fool some of the people some of the time, but not all of the people all of the time.

40. Actions speak louder than words.

41. Sticks and stones may break my bones but words will never hurt me.

42. If the shoe fits, wear it.

43. A man's home is his castle.

44. In this company, we work half-days — any 12 hours you prefer.

45. Better safe than sorry.

46. You can't take it with you.

47. Don't cross the bridge until you get to it.

48. Beauty is in the eye of the beholder.

49. There are two sides to every story.

50. It's always darkest just before the dawn.

51. The eyes are the window to the soul.

52. Once a man, twice a boy.

53. Every great story needs telling.

54. You can't judge a book by its cover.

55. We always hurt the ones we love.

56. One man's trash is another man's treasure.

57. Bet it all, sleep in the dirty hall.

58. Slow and steady wins the race.

59. The cream always rises to the top.

60. It's just as easy to sell a Rolls-Royce as it is to sell a Chevy — and you don't have to sell as many.

61. Don't let grass grow under your feet.

62. You don't get respect if your back is not erect.

63. It is more blessed to give than to receive.

64. A good scare is worth more than good advice.

65. Wait to worry.

66. Every man is his own worst enemy.

67. It is the mark of an educated mind to be able to entertain a thought without accepting it. (Aristotle)

68. When the music starts, get up and dance or go home.

69. True love never grows old.

70. Never look a gift horse in the mouth.

71. Better a thousand enemies outside the house than one inside.

72. A chain is no stronger than its weakest link.

73. God helps those who help themselves.

74. There's always room at the top.

75. Nothing ventured, nothing gained.

76. Absence makes the heart grow fonder.

77. When we point the finger at someone, there are always three pointing back at us.

78. An honest man's word is as good as his bond.

79. History repeats itself.

80. The family that prays together stays together.

81. It's not how much money you earn that counts, but rather how much you have when you need it.

82. The road to hell is paved with good intentions.

83. Laughter is the best medicine.

84. Self-praise is no recommendation.

85. Great oaks from little acorns grow.

86. A nod is as good as a wink to a blind horse.

87. Books and friends should be few but good.

88. Never do things by halves.

89. In the land of the blind, the one-eyed man is king.

90. To deceive oneself is very easy.

91. He who hesitates is lost.

92. A liar is worse than a thief.

93. Attitude is more important than aptitude in determining altitude.

94. Two heads are better than one.

95. Out of debt, out of danger.

96. When one door shuts, another opens.

97. We must learn to walk before we can run.

98. Let sleeping dogs lie.

99. An hour in the morning is worth two in the evening.

100. Life is sweet.

101. A promise made is a debt unpaid.

Wisdom From the Holy Bible

This section includes helpful verses from the Bible (New International Version) selected by BIC Alliance and its friends, marketing partners and *BIC Magazine* readers.

Old Testament

Give generously to him and do so without a grudging heart; then because of this the Lord your God will bless you in all your work and in everything you put your hand to. There will always be poor people in the land. Therefore I command you to be openhanded toward your brothers and toward the poor and needy in your land.
Deuteronomy 15:10-11

At Gibeon the Lord appeared to Solomon during the night in a dream, and God said, "Ask for whatever you want me to give you." Solomon answered, "You have shown great kindness to your servant, my father David, because he was faithful to you and righteous and upright in heart. You have continued this great kindness to him and have given him a son to sit on his throne this very day.

"Now, O Lord my God, you have made your servant king in place of my father David. But I am only a little child and do not know how to carry out my duties. Your servant is here among the people you have chosen, a great people, too numerous to count or number. So give your servant a discerning heart to govern your people and to distinguish between right and wrong. For who is able to govern this great people of yours?"

The Lord was pleased that Solomon had asked for this. So God said to him, "Since you have asked for this and not for long life or wealth for yourself, nor have asked for the death of your enemies but for discernment in administering justice, I will do what you have asked. I will give you a wise and discerning heart, so that there will never have been anyone like you, nor will there ever be. Moreover, I will give you what you have not asked for — both riches and honor — so that in your lifetime you will have no equal among kings."
1 Kings 3:5-13

He spoke three thousand proverbs and his songs numbered a thousand and five.
1 Kings 4:32

The Lord makes me lie down in green pastures, he leads me beside quiet waters, he restores my soul. He guides me in my paths of righteousness for his name's sake.
Psalm 23:2-3

187

Even though I walk through the valley of the shadow of death/I will fear no evil, for you are with me/your rod and your staff, they comfort me.
Psalm 23:4

May those who delight in my vindication shout for joy and gladness; may they always say, "The Lord be exalted, who delights in the well-being of his servant."
Psalm 35:27

Create in me a clean heart, O God, and renew a steadfast spirit within me. Do not cast me away from Your presence, and do not take Your Holy Spirit from me. Restore to me the joy of Your salvation, and uphold me [by Your] generous Spirit. [Then] I will teach transgressors Your ways, and sinners shall be converted to You.
Psalm 51:10-13

Praise the Lord. Give thanks to the Lord, for he is good; his love endures forever.
Psalm 106:1

This is the day which the Lord has made; Let us rejoice and be glad in it.
Psalm 118:24

My son, if you accept my words and store up my commands within you, turning your ear to wisdom and applying your heart to understanding, and if you call out for insight and cry aloud for understanding, and if you look for it as for silver and search for it as for hidden treasure, then you will understand the fear of the Lord and find the knowledge of God.
Proverbs 2:1-5

Let love and faithfulness never leave you; bind them around your neck, write them on a tablet in your heart. Then you will win favor in the sight of God and man.
Proverbs 3:3-4

Trust in the Lord with all your heart and lean not on your own understanding; in all your ways acknowledge him, and he will make your paths straight.
Proverbs 3:5-6

Honor the Lord with your wealth, with the firstfruits of all your crops; then your barns will be filled to overflowing, and your vats will brim over with new wine.
Proverbs 3:9-10

Instruct a wise man and he will be wiser still; teach a righteous man and he will add to his learning.
Proverbs 9:9

The man of integrity walks securely, but he who takes crooked paths will be found out.
Proverbs 10:9

A fool finds pleasure in evil conduct, but a man of understanding delights in wisdom.
Proverbs 10:23

When pride comes, then comes disgrace, but with humility comes wisdom.
Proverbs 11:2

A generous man will prosper; he who refreshes others will himself be refreshed.
Proverbs 11:25

He who works his land will have abundant food but he who chases fantasies lacks judgment.
Proverbs 12:11

The ways of a fool seem right to him, but a wise man listens to advice.
Proverbs 12:15

He who guards his lips guards his life, but he who speaks rashly will come to ruin.
Proverbs 13:3

He who walks with the wise grows wise, but a companion of fools suffers harm.
Proverbs 13:20

Better a little with righteousness than much gain with injustice.
Proverbs 16:8

Listen to advice and accept instruction, and in the end you will be wise.
Proverbs 19:20

A good name is more desirable than great riches; to be esteemed is better than silver or gold.
Proverbs 22:1

Train a child in the way he should go, and when he is old he will not turn from it.
Proverbs 22:6

As iron sharpens iron, so one man sharpens another.
Proverbs 27:17

Where there is no revelation, the people cast off restraint; but blessed is he who keeps the law.
Proverbs 29:18

A wife of noble character who can find? She is worth more than rubies. Her husband has full confidence in her and lacks nothing in value. She brings him good not harm all the days of his life.
Proverbs 31:10-12

Charm is deceptive, and beauty is fleeting, but the woman who fears the Lord is to be praised.
Proverbs 31:30

Two are better than one because they have a good return for their work. If one falls down, his friend can help him up. But pity the man who falls and has no one to help him up! Also, if two lie down together, they will keep warm. But how can one keep warm alone? Though one may be overpowered, two can defend themselves. A cord of three strands is not quickly broken.
Ecclesiastes 4:9-12

Moreover, when God gives any man wealth and possessions, and enables him to enjoy them, to accept his lot and be happy in his work — this is a gift of God.
Ecclesiastes 5:19

The quiet words of the wise are more to be heeded than the shouts of a ruler of fools.
Ecclesiastes 9:17

So do not fear, for I am with you; do not be dismayed, for I am your God. I will strengthen you and help you; I will uphold you with my righteous right hand.
Isaiah 41:10

This is what the Lord says — your Redeemer, the Holy One of Israel: "I am the LORD your God, who teaches you what is best for you, who directs you in the way you should go."
Isaiah 48:17

Come, all you who are thirsty, come to the waters; and you who have no money, come, buy and eat! Come, buy wine and milk without money and without cost. Why spend money on what is not bread, and your labor on what does not satisfy? Listen, listen to me, and eat what is good, and your soul will delight in the richest of fare. Give ear and come to me; hear me, that your soul may live. I will make an everlasting covenant with you, my faithful love promised to David.
Isaiah 55:1-3

"For my thoughts are not your thoughts, neither are your ways my ways," declares the Lord.
Isaiah 55:8

"For I know the plans I have for you," declares the Lord, "plans to prosper you and not to harm you, plans to give you hope and a future. Then you will call upon me and come and pray to me, and I will listen to you. You will seek me and find me when you seek me with all your heart."
Jeremiah 29:11-13

"Bring the whole tithe into the storehouse, that there may be food in my house. Test me in this," says the Lord Almighty, "and see if I will not throw open the floodgates of heaven and pour out so much blessing that you will not have room enough for it."
Malachi 3:10

New Testament

Blessed are the poor in spirit, for theirs is the kingdom of heaven. Blessed are those who mourn, for they will be comforted. Blessed are the meek, for they will inherit the earth. Blessed are those who hunger and thirst for righteousness, for they will be filled. Blessed are the merciful, for they will be shown mercy. Blessed are the pure in heart, for they will see God. Blessed are the peacemakers, for they will be called sons of God. Blessed are those who are persecuted because of righteousness, for theirs is the kingdom of heaven.

Blessed are you when people insult you, persecute you and falsely say all kinds of evil against you because of me.
Matthew 5:3-11

This, then, is how you should pray: "Our Father in heaven, hallowed be your name, your kingdom come, your will be done on earth as it is in heaven. Give us today our daily bread. Forgive us our debts, as we also have forgiven our debtors. And lead us not into temptation, but deliver us from the evil one."
Matthew 6:9-13

Jesus said, "If you forgive men when they sin against you, your heavenly Father will also forgive you."
Matthew 6:14

No one can serve two masters. Either he will hate the one and love the other, or he will be devoted to the one and despise the other. You cannot serve both God and Money.
Matthew 6:24

But seek first his kingdom and his righteousness, and all these things will be given to you as well.
Matthew 6:33

Therefore do not worry about tomorrow, for tomorrow will worry about itself. Each day has enough trouble of its own.
Matthew 6:34

Do not judge or you too will be judged. For in the same way you judge others you will be judged, and with the measures you use, it will be measured to you. Why do you look at the speck in your brother's eye and pay no attention to the plank in your own eye?
Matthew 7:1-3

Ask, and it will be given to you; seek and you will find; knock and the door will be opened to you. For everyone who asks receives, he who seeks finds and to him who knocks the door will be open.
Matthew 7:7-8

So in everything, do to others what you would have them do to you, for this sums up the Law and the Prophets.
Matthew 7:12

The Son of Man came eating and drinking, and they say, "Here is a glutton and a drunkard, a friend of tax collectors and sinners." But wisdom is proved right by her actions.
Matthew 11:19

Come to me, all you who are weary and burdened, and I will give you rest. Take my yoke upon you and learn from me, for I am gentle and humble in heart, and you will find rest for your souls. For my yoke is easy and my burden is light.
Matthew 11:28-30

Jesus replied: "Love the Lord your God with all your heart and with all your soul and with all your mind." This is the first and greatest commandment. And the second is like it: "Love your neighbor as yourself." All the Law and the Prophets hang on these two commandments.
Matthew 22:37-40

The King will reply, "I tell you the truth, whatever you did for one of the least of

these brothers of mine, you did for me."
Matthew 25:40

"From childhood," he answered. "It has often thrown him into fire or water to kill him. But if you can do anything, take pity on us and help us."

"If you can?" said Jesus. "Everything is possible for him who believes."

Immediately the boy's father exclaimed, "I do believe; help me overcome my unbelief!"
Mark 9:22-24

Jesus said to them, "Go into all the world and preach the good news to all creation. Whoever believes and is baptized will be saved, but whoever does not believe will be condemned."
Mark 16:15-16

Do not judge and you will not be judged. Do not condemn and you will not be condemned. Forgive and you will be forgiven. Give and it will be given to you. A good measure pressed down, shaken together and running over will be poured into your lap. For with the measure you use, it will be measured to you.
Luke 6:37-38

Jesus said to them, "Watch out! Be on your guard against all kinds of greed; a man's life does not consist in the abundance of his possessions."
Luke 12:15

Jesus said, "You must also be ready, because the Son of Man will come at an hour when you do not expect him."
Luke 12:40

Jesus declared, "I tell you the truth, no one can see the kingdom of Heaven unless he is born again."
John 3:3

God so loved the world that he gave his one and only Son, that whoever believes in him shall not perish but have eternal life.
John 3:16

For God did not send his Son into the world to condemn the world, but to save the world through him.
John 3:17

To this John replied, "A man can receive only what is given him from heaven."
John 3:27

Jesus declared, "I am the bread of life. He who comes to me will never go hungry, and he who believes in me will never go thirsty."
John 6:35

When Jesus spoke to the people he said, "I am the light of the world. Whoever follows me will never walk in darkness, but will have the light of life."
John 8:12

The thief comes only to steal and kill and destroy; I have come that they may have life, and have it to the full.
John 10:10

Jesus said to her, "I am the resurrection and the life. He who believes in me will live, even though he dies; and whoever lives and believes in me will never die."
John 11:25-26

Jesus said, "By this all men will know that you are my disciples, if you love one another."
John 13:35

Jesus said, "In my Father's house are many rooms; if it were not so, I would have told you. I am going there to prepare a place for you. And if I go and prepare a place for you, I will come back and take you to be with me that you may also be where I am."
John 14:2-3

Jesus replied, "If anyone loves me, he will obey my teaching. My Father will love him, and we will come to him and make our home with him."
John 14:23

The wages of sin is death, but the gift of God is eternal life in Christ Jesus our Lord.
Romans 6:23

Therefore, there is now no condemnation for those who are in Christ Jesus.
Romans 8:1

Do not conform any longer to the pattern of this world, but be transformed by the renewing of your mind. Then you will be able to test and approve what God's will is — his good, pleasing and perfect will.
Romans 12:2

Let no doubt remain outstanding, except the continuing debt to love one another, for he who loves his fellowman has fulfilled the law.
Romans 13:8

Love is patient, love is kind. It does not envy, it does not boast, it is not proud. It is not rude, it is not self-seeking, it is not easily angered, it keeps no record of wrongs. Love does not delight in evil but rejoices with the truth. It always protects, always trusts, always hopes, always perseveres.
1 Corinthians 13:4-7

When I was a child, I talked like a child, I thought like a child, I reasoned like a child. When I became a man, I put childish ways behind me.
1 Corinthians 13:11

The entire law is summed up in a single command: "Love your neighbor as yourself."
Galatians 5:14

But because of his great love for us, God, who is rich in mercy, made us alive with Christ even when we were dead in transgressions — it is by grace you have been saved.
Ephesians 2:4-5

For this reason I kneel before the Father, from whom his whole family in heaven and on earth derives its name. I pray that out of his glorious riches he may strengthen you with power through his Spirit in your inner being, so that Christ may dwell in your hearts through faith. And I pray that you, being rooted and established in love, may have power, together with all the saints, to grasp how wide and long and high and deep is the love of Christ, and to know this love that surpasses knowledge — that you may be filled to the measure of all the fullness of God. Now to him who is able to do immeasurably more than all we ask or imagine, according to his power that is at work within us.
Ephesians 3:14-20

Do nothing out of selfish ambition or vain conceit, but in humility consider others better than yourselves.
Philippians 2:3

And being found in appearance as a man, he humbled himself and became obedient to death — even death on a cross!
Philippians 2:8

Do not be anxious about anything, but in everything, by prayer and petition, with thanksgiving, present your requests to God. And the peace of God, which transcends all understanding, will guard your hearts and your minds in Christ Jesus. Finally, brothers, whatever is true, whatever is noble, whatever is right, whatever is pure, whatever is lovely, whatever is admirable — if anything is excellent or praiseworthy — think about such things.
Philippians 4:6-8

I can do everything through him who gives me strength.
Philippians 4:13

Therefore, as God's chosen people, holy and dearly loved, clothe yourselves with compassion, kindness, humility, gentleness and patience.
Colossians 3:12

And whatever you do, whether in word or deed, do it all in the name of the Lord Jesus, giving thanks to God the Father through him.
Colossians 3:17

And the things you have heard me say in the presence of many witnesses entrust to reliable men who will also be qualified to teach others.
2 Timothy 2:2

I have fought the good fight, I have finished the race, I have kept the faith. Now there is in store for me the crown of righteousness, which the Lord, the righteous Judge, will award me on that day — and not only to me, but also to all who have longed for his appearing.
2 Timothy 4:7-8

Because Christ himself suffered when he was tempted, he is able to help those being tempted.
Hebrews 2:18

Faith is being sure of what we hope for and certain of what we do not see.
Hebrews 11:1

No discipline seems pleasant at the time, but painful. Later on, however, it produces a harvest of righteousness and peace for those who have been trained by it.
Hebrews 12:11

Make every effort to be at peace with all men and to be holy; without holiness no one will see the Lord.
Hebrews 12:14

Keep your lives free from the love of money and be content with what you have, because God has said, "Never will I leave you; never will I forsake you."
Hebrews 13:5

Perseverance must finish its work so that you may be mature and complete, not lacking anything.
James 1:4

Don't be deceived, my dear brothers. Every good and perfect gift is from above, coming down from the Father of the heavenly lights, who does not change like shifting shadows.
James 1:16-17

In the same way, faith by itself, if it is not accompanied by action, is dead.
James 2:17

Who is wise and understanding among you? Let him show it by his good life, by deeds done in the humility that comes from wisdom. But if you harbor bitter envy and selfish ambition in your hearts, do not boast about it or deny the truth. Such "wisdom" does not come down from heaven but is earthly, unspiritual, of the devil. For where you have envy and selfish ambition, there you find disorder and every evil practice.

But the wisdom that comes from heaven is first of all pure; then peace-loving, considerate, submissive, full of mercy and good fruit, impartial and sincere. Peacemakers who sow in peace raise a harvest of righteousness.
James 3:13-18

To him who loves us and has freed us from our sins by his blood, and has made us to be a kingdom and priests to serve his God and Father — to him be glory and power forever and ever! Amen.
Revelation 1:5-6

He said to me: "It is done. I am the Alpha and the Omega, the Beginning and the End. To him who is thirsty I will give to drink without cost from the spring of the water of life. He who overcomes will inherit all this, and I will be his God and he will be my son."
Revelation 21:6-7

50 Tips for Greater Peace, Happiness and Success

By Earl Heard

1. Join and become active in the organizations related to your profession.
2. Focus on being more interested instead of being more interesting.
3. Treat others as you would like to be treated instead of treating them the way they treat you.
4. Learn and practice the art of listening.
5. More people become successful because they're nice than because they're brilliant.
6. A smiling face is the best way to end a conversation or a written personal note.
7. Keep good business and personal financial records.
8. Save regularly.
9. Learn and practice the art of networking by making three excellent referrals per day.
10. Keep a business journal and a family journal and review them regularly.
11. When mistakes happen, learn from them.
12. Don't be afraid of hard work. It won't kill you.
13. Set written business and personal goals — daily, weekly, monthly and annually.
14. If you supervise others, know and review their goals at least monthly.
15. Practice what you preach. No one likes a hypocrite.
16. Practice safety and environmental consciousness on the job and off.
17. Become a positive role model at work and at home.
18. Before speaking, think about how the person listening will interpret what you say.
19. Encourage others instead of putting them down.
20. Never stop learning.
21. Don't discriminate toward others on the basis of race, color, religion or economic status.
22. Seek mentors for yourself and become a mentor to others.
23. Listen to motivational speakers, tapes, preachers, etc.
24. Learn and practice effective time management techniques.
25. Learn how to dress and dine properly.
26. Learn and practice good verbal communication skills.
27. Thank people regularly for their business, help, etc.
28. Surround yourself with honest, ethical and hardworking people.
29. Stay away from negative people, places and situations.
30. Before you evaluate others, ask them to evaluate their own performance.

31. Build a library of motivational/how-to books and magazines and read them.
32. Practice self control in all that you say and do.
33. Practice presentations before making them. A great way to do this is to videotape yourself making a presentation or watch yourself in a mirror acting as both the buyer and the seller.
34. When speaking or making a presentation, be prepared for anything or any question that might arise.
35. Research and prospecting are the keys to successful entrepreneurship and sales.
36. It's not "see more and you'll sell more" — it's more about prospecting better and then seeing more of the best prospects.
37. Remember what it was like at the bottom, and help others reach the next rung on the ladder of success.
38. Get involved in your community's activities.
39. Remember, Abe Lincoln lost many elections before becoming a winner. Never give up!
40. Learn to master nonverbal communication to influence others — facial expressions, tone of voice, listening, etc. Since 90 percent of our communication is nonverbal, it's important to remember that actions speak louder than words.
41. Preview before you begin a meeting, and review after you finish a meeting.
42. Give praise in public. Criticism, however, should be done in private, even when it's constructive in nature.
43. One of the great things about starting at the bottom is that there is plenty of room to advance.
44. The best way to build self-confidence is to know how to act properly and say the right things at the right time.
45. Compromise is better than confrontation. Find the middle ground where everyone is comfortable.
46. True success comes when we've reached the point where we are more concerned with doing what's right than obtaining money, publicity and/or recognition.
47. Before we can manage others effectively, we must master self-management.
48. Marketing is like stepping up to bat, and sales is like hitting the ball out of the park.
49. The best friend you can have in business is someone who buys ink by the barrel.
50. Remember — it's what we do together that counts!

Part VI:

Lagniappe

"My whole life, my whole soul, my whole spirit is to blow that horn."

— Louis Armstrong

About BIC Alliance

The mission of BIC Alliance is to connect people in business, industry and community with one another for the betterment of all.

The story of BIC Alliance began when Earl Heard first conceived the idea for an industry publication that, unlike others that existed at the time, would cover all sectors of the energy business. As a former training manager for Ethyl Corp. in Baton Rouge, La., Heard used his knowledge of the buying process and the contacts he had made over the years to develop a unique formula that would enable suppliers to reach a wide variety of industries for a minimal investment. Heard launched *The Training Coordinator* — the first training publication in industry — in 1981. Three years later, it would evolve into *BIC Magazine*.

Today, *BIC Magazine* stands as the Western Hemisphere's largest multi-industry, multidepartmental energy publication, featuring the latest news and issues related to the oil and gas, power generation, construction, and pulp and paper industries. The publication reaches approximately 120,000 readers, including industry professionals in the United States and 55 other countries. Each issue of *BIC Magazine* can be read in its entirety at www.bicalliance.com.

BIC Magazine is unique in that it offers BIC Alliance marketing partners a holistic approach to reaching key industry decision makers through several components, including advertising, case histories/PR, direct mail and custom data selection.

IVS Investment Banking

IVS Investment Banking is the merger and acquisition intermediary arm of BIC Alliance. Founded in 1994, IVS is a boutique investment bank primarily servicing sell side transactions in the industrial space in which *BIC Magazine* operates.

IVS can help interested parties with:
• Management-led buyouts.
• Buying or selling a company.
• Leveraged recapitalization.
• Raising capital to grow.

Because we're in the publishing business, oftentimes IVS knows the news before it is news. In many cases, IVS enjoys a longstanding, trusting business relationship with business owners who are only now considering an exit strategy or firms seeking either to expand geographically or expand their service lines. IVS began as a "business cupid" linking buyers and sellers of businesses together.

Today, IVS offers complete investment banking services to help buy, sell or grow companies in the industrial marketplace. With the ability to access an unprecedented number of industry executives, IVS has the knowledge and experience necessary to complete a number of investment banking services, delivering premium value for business owners.

IVS Investment Banking works with management teams in acquiring manufacturing, distribution and service oriented businesses in the petrochemical, refining, power generation, construction, marine, and pulp and paper industries. Over the course of their careers, IVS' principals have worked on M&A transactions whose aggregate value has totaled in excess of $1 billion.

BIC Recruiting

BIC Alliance's talent acquisition division helps recruit the best of the best in management, operations, and sales and marketing professionals for its clients. The division's first placement was in 1999, when Ben Kupka joined Keibler-Thompson in an engineering and sales position. Since that time, the company's proven record of finding the right people for the right jobs has convinced business leaders to use BIC Recruiting for their placement needs.

BIC Recruiting's focus is on sales and marketing management, general management with P&L expertise and mid- and senior-level sales executives. BIC Recruiting also has expertise in placement of marketing, operations, engineering and environmental, health and safety professionals. Lastly, by working with our investment banking affiliate, BIC Recruiting has expertise in the placement of C-level executives for employers in existing as well as new positions where mergers and acquisitions have occurred.

BIC Alliance has an extensive network of more than 27,000 contacts that allows us to fill a variety of positions throughout industry. The network is used as a starting point for a proactive targeted search for the best candidates for a particular position. BIC Recruiting conducts screening and reference checks,

206

arranges interviews and provides any necessary candidate assessment tools that allow the employer to assure that a good fit will occur for both employer and candidate.

BIC Media Solutions

BIC Media Solutions is a fully integrated communication, training and event planning division within BIC Alliance. The mission of BIC Media Solutions is to offer a broader range of multimedia communication and training services to BIC Alliance's marketing partners and readers, including custom book publishing; creative services; human performance improvement in the areas of management, marketing and sales via seminars; and event planning services for trade shows, conferences, and networking and hospitality events.

Founded in 2005, BIC Publishing is the custom book publishing division of BIC Alliance. It offers turnkey production or upgrading of sales, marketing, management and operations training materials needed to help your business run better. BIC Publishing services include copywriting, editing, ghostwriting, layout, design, marketing and publicity. The company also partners with the best printers and distributors in the business to see the project through in a way that is friendly to your budget, from concept to reader.

BIC Publishing has previously produced three books — *It's What We Do Together That Counts: The BIC Alliance Story, Energy Entrepreneurs* and *Industry Achievers*.

BIC Alliance Marketing Partners, 2009-10

BIC Alliance would like to thank its marketing partners for their support in 2009 and 2010, which has made it possible for us to make *BIC Magazine* the Western Hemisphere's largest multi-industry, multidepartmental energy publication and publish this book. Please consider these companies' products and services when selecting suppliers. This list is continually growing, so visit www.bicalliance. com for the most up-to-date information.

24HR SAFETY
3-J RYAN INC.
360TRAINING.COM
3E NDT
5 STAR OUTFITTERS
A BOX 4 U
AARON OIL CO.
ABC HOUSTON
ABS CONSULTING
ACADIAN WASTE DISPOSAL
ACS INDUSTRIES LP
ADT ADVANCED INTEGRATION
ADVANCED COMPRESSOR TECHNOLOGY
ADVANCED OFFICE SYSTEMS
ADVANCED TEST EQUIPMENT
AEROTEK
AGGREGATE TECHNOLOGIES INC.
AGGREKO
AGGRESSIVE EQUIPMENT
ALLIANCE PASTEX
AMERICAN SOCIETY OF
 SAFETY ENGINEERS
AMISTCO SEPARATION PRODUCTS
APACHE OIL CO.
APPLICATION FACTORY
AQUA DRILL INTERNATIONAL
AQUA SALES
ASHTEAD TECHNOLOGY RENTALS
ASME PEM TRADE SHOW
ASNT–THE GREATER HOUSTON SECTION
ASNT/AMERICAN SOCIETY FOR
 NONDESTRUCTIVE TESTING
ATEC STEEL FABRICATION
 & CONSTRUCTION
ATLANTIC INDUSTRIAL

ATLAS COPCO PRIME ENERGY
AUSTIN INDUSTRIAL
AVIDA AMERICAS
AZTEC BOLTING SERVICES INC.
AZTEC TENTS AND EVENTS
BAKER PETROLITE
BAKER PRINTING/KEEPSAFE
BAKERCORP
BBB TANK SERVICES
BEALINE SERVICE CO.
BETCO SCAFFOLDS
BETTER PUMPS & SOLUTIONS
BGI CONTRACTORS
BIZZUKA
BOWEN, MICLETTE & BRITT
BRAND ENERGY & INFRASTRUCTURE
 SERVICES
BROCK GROUP, THE
CAM ENVIRONMENTAL SERVICES
CANONGATE GOLF CLUBS
CAP5 TECHNOLOGY SOLUTIONS
CAPPS
CAREER BUILDERS OF LOUISIANA
CARLTON INDUSTRIES
CAROL CRANE RIGGING & LIFTING
 TECHNOLOGY INC.
CASHCO VCI
CAT ENERGY RENTAL SOLUTIONS
CAT TECH INC.
CBG MAINTENANCE SERVICES
CERTIFIEDSAFETY SPECIALISTS
CHECKPOINT PROCESS PUMPS
 & SYSTEMS
CHEMTECH CHEMICAL SERVICES
CID ASSOCIATES

CINATRA CLEAN TECHNOLOGIES INC.
CLEAN HARBORS ENVIRONMENTAL
  SERVICES
COASTAL REFRACTORY SERVICES
COATING & APPLICATION SERVICES
COMMERCIAL FENCE & ACCESS
  CONTROLS
CONTRACT RESOURCES
COT-PURITECH
CPI SALES ASSOCIATES LLC
CREATIVE RESOURCES GROUP
C.S. UNITEC
CUDD ENERGY SERVICES
DEHUMIDIFICATION
  TECHNOLOGIES INC.
DELTA RIGGING & TOOLS
DELTA VALVE USA
DELTAK MANUFACTURING INC.
DETCON INC.
DISA INC.
DIVERSIFIED BUSINESS
  COMMUNICATIONS
DRIFIRE
EAGLE SWS
EMPIRE SCAFFOLD
EMSI (EMISSION MONITORING
  SERVICE INC.)
ENERGY SERVICES INTERNATIONAL
ENVIROCON
EP MONITORING
EQ - THE ENVIRONMENTAL
  QUALITY COMPANY
ES&H CONSULTING SERVICES
ETEN
EURO PETROLEUM CONSULTANTS LTD.
EVEREADY ENERGY SERVICES
EVERGREEN INDUSTRIAL SERVICES
EXCEL GROUP
EXCEL MODULAR SCAFFOLD & LEASING
EXPANSION JOINT SYSTEMS
FABENCO INC.
FIRST ADVANTAGE CORP.
FISHBONE COMPANIES
FLARE IGNITORS PIPELINE &
  REFINERY LLC

FLOW INTERNATIONAL CORP.
FURMANITE USA
GALLAGHER SECURITY MANAGEMENT
  SYSTEMS
GARDAWORLD
GATORWORKS
GEM MOBILE TREATMENT SERVICES
GEORGE H. BODMAN INC.
GLOBAL WRAP LLC
GLOVE GUARD LP
GORMAN-RUPP
GREAT WESTERN METALS
GROWTH CAPITAL PARTNERS
GULF SOUTH ROTATING MACHINERY
  SYMPOSIUM
GULF SOUTH SCAFFOLDING
HAGEMEYER NORTH AMERICA
HARRINGTON HOISTS
HEMCO
HERTZ EQUIPMENT RENTAL CORP.
HILTON HOUSTON HOBBY AIRPORT
HITEMCO
HOUSTON AREA SAFETY COUNCIL
HOUSTON COATING SOCIETY
HUNTER BUILDINGS &
  MANUFACTURING
HYATT PLACE
HYDRATIGHT
HYTORC
IMPACT MARKETING
INCREASE PERFORMANCE
INDUMAR PRODUCTS INC.
INDUSTRIAL BLIND SOLUTIONS
INDUSTRIAL EMERGENCY
  SERVICES LLC
INDUSTRIAL FIRE WORLD
INDUSTRIAL GUNITE INC.
INDUSTRIAL PERFORMANCE SERVICES
INDUSTRIAL SAFETY
  TRAINING COUNCIL
INDUSTRIAL SURFACING CORP.
INDUSTRY VISIONS
INLAND INDUSTRIAL SERVICES GROUP
INNOVATIVE EHS INC.
INTERNATIONAL LIQUID TERMINALS

ASSOCIATION
INTRA-SERVICES
ISO PANELS INC.
JAMMIE'S ENVIRONMENTAL INC.
JEFFERSON PARISH ECONOMIC
  DEVELOPMENT COMMISSION
JUNIPER SYSTEMS
JV INDUSTRIAL COMPANIES LTD
KAP PROJECT SERVICES
KBR
KBC ADVANCED TECHNOLOGIES INC.
KMAC SPECIALTY SERVICES INC.
KMT WATERJET SYSTEMS
KNIGHTHAWK ENGINEERING
KTI CORP.
LA BAYOU BISTRO/ASHLEY MANOR
LAMONS
LAYHER
LIFTING GEAR HIRE CORP.
LOUISIANA DEPARTMENT OF ECONOMIC
DEVELOPMENT
LUDECA INC.
LUNKER LODGE
MAINTENANCE ENTERPRISES INC.
MANAGEMENT CONTROLS INC.
MANUFACTURING GAME, THE
MARRIOTT NEW ORLEANS
MASCOAT PRODUCTS
MASS TECHNOLOGY CORP.
MATHEY DEARMAN
MATRIX SERVICE
MB INDUSTRIES
MEDICAL PLAZA MOBILE
  SURVEILLANCE
MESA PRODUCTS
MHT ACCESS SERVICES INC.
MOBLEY INDUSTRIAL SERVICES INC.
MOODY GARDENS HOTEL
MOURIK LP
MOXIE MEDIA
MPRINT ADVERTISING SPECIALTIES
MTS
MUNDY COMPANIES
MUSTANG ENGINEERING
NACE INTERNATIONAL

NATIONAL CENTER FOR CONSTRUCTION
  EDUCATION AND RESEARCH
NATIONAL SAFETY COUNCIL
NEPTUNE RESEARCH INC.
NIMLOK LOUISIANA
NLB CORP.
NOTTOWAY PLANTATION
NPRA
ODOM INDUSTRIES
OHMSTEDE INDUSTRIAL SERVICES
OILIND SAFETY
OLYMPUS NDT
PARAMED SYSTEMS
PARKER HANNIFIN CORP.
PATENT CONSTRUCTION SYSTEMS
PENNWELL (POWERGEN
  INTERNATIONAL)
PETRO-VALVE INC.
PETROCHEM DATA SERVICES
PETROSPECT INSPECTION SERVICES
PHYSICAL ACOUSTICS CORP.
PLANT MAINTENANCE SERVICES/EPSCO
PORTAGAS
POSEIDON
PRIDE MANAGEMENT
PROACT SAFETY INC.
PROCESS AND INDUSTRY PRACTICES
  (PIP)
PSI/PETROCHEMICAL SERVICES INC.
QSA GLOBAL
RABALAIS I&E CONSTRUCTORS
RAE SYSTEMS
RAM TECHNOLOGY GROUP
REPCONSTRICKLAND
ROBERT J. JENKINS & CO.
ROCO RESCUE
RSC EQUIPMENT RENTAL
RUGGED CYCLES
RYDLYME
SAFETY COUNCIL OF LA CAPITAL AREA
SAFETY HOUSE
SAFETY MANAGEMENT SYSTEMS
SAFEWORKS
SAFWAY SERVICES
SATELLITE SHELTERS INC.

211

SCAFFOLDING TODAY
SELAS FLUID
SHUTDOWNS–TURNAROUNDS–OUTAGES
 (STO 2009)
SOCIETY FOR PROTECTIVE
 COATINGS, THE
SOUTHEAST TEXAS INDUSTRIES INC.
SOUTH SHORE HARBOUR RESORT AND
 CONFERENCE CENTER
SOUTHWEST EQUIPMENT RENTALS INC.
SPARKLING CLEAR INDUSTRIES
SPEED INDUSTRIAL SERVICES
SPIR STAR
SPRINT INDUSTRIAL
SPX COOLING TECHNOLOGIES
SPX HYDRAULIC TECHNOLOGIES
STARCON INTERNATIONAL INC.
STEPUP SCAFFOLDING LLC
STRESS ENGINEERING SERVICES
STRUCTURAL GROUP
SUCCESS IMAGES
SUN COAST RESOURCES INC.
SUPERHEAT FGH SERVICES INC.
SUPRIYA JINDAL FOUNDATION
 FOR LOUISIANA'S CHILDREN
SWIFT INTERNATIONAL SERVICE GROUP
TAPCO ENPRO
TAPER-LOK CORP.
T.D. WILLIAMSON INC.
TEAM INDUSTRIAL SERVICES
TEEX EMERGENCY SERVICES TRAINING
 INSTITUTE
TEPCO
TEPSCO LP
TESTO INC.
TEX STAR MARKETING
TEXAS ACG CAPITAL CONNECTION
TEXAS ALLIANCE OF
 ENERGY PRODUCERS
TEXAS GULF COAST ENGINEERS
TEXAS INDUSTRIAL SPECIALTIES
TEXAS RENAISSANCE FESTIVAL
THOMPSON PUMP
TIE OFF 100
TIGER INDUSTRIAL RENTALS

TIMEC
TOADFLY
TORQUE TOOLS INC.
TOTAL SAFETY
TRADEFAIR GROUP, THE
TRAINING & DEVELOPMENT
 SYSTEMS INC.
TRAY-TEC INC.
TRISTAR GLOBAL ENERGY SOLUTIONS
TRITON INDUSTRIES
TURBOMACHINERY LABORATORY
TURNAROUND MANAGEMENT
 COMPANY, THE
TURNER INDUSTRIES
UHP PROJECTS INC.
UNITED ENVIRONMENTAL SERVICES
UNITED RENTALS
UNITED STATES INDUSTRIAL SERVICES
UNIVERSAL PLANT SERVICES INC.
VAPOR POINT
VEOLIA ES INDUSTRIAL SERVICES
VIDISCO LTD.
VPPPA
VPPPA REGION VI
VULCAN FINNED TUBES
WATERJET TECHNOLOGY ASSOCIATION
WINGATE PARTNERS
WOLF CREEK BUSINESS
 GROWTH INSTITUTE
WOODY FALGOUST
WYATT FIELD SERVICE CO.

What People Have to Say About BIC Alliance, IVS Investment Banking, BIC Recruiting and BIC Publishing

At BIC Alliance, we are strong believers in the use of third-party testimonials in an effective strategic marketing campaign. Many of BIC Alliance's marketing partners have gone on record to say how their campaigns and use of the services mentioned above have helped them achieve greater market share, top-of-mind awareness and closer relationships with industrial buyers and suppliers. In addition, readers of BIC Publishing's four books — *It's What We Do Together That Counts*, *Energy Entrepreneurs*, *Industry Achievers* and *Earl's Pearls* — have shared their thoughts about how the stories of hard work and success have shaped their lives.

Robert Lasser, national sales manager for ACS Industries, on *BIC Magazine*:

"We have used BIC Alliance's marketing services for several years and plan to continue utilizing their services. ACS has received strong response to our advertising campaigns in BIC Magazine. BIC Alliance always goes the extra mile by helping us gather, qualify and publish guest articles, customer testimonies and case studies. We have also participated in several BIC Alliance networking events and they have provided us with many direct referrals. We have been very pleased with the whole team at BIC Alliance and would recommend them strongly."

Scott Thibodeaux of Gulf South Scaffolding Inc. on *BIC Magazine* and BIC Recruiting:

"I have used BIC Magazine for marketing for more than 10 years during my career and have received tangible results. As a result of my first campaign, I received an initiative with an $8 million a year revenue potential.

"I chose to use BIC Recruiting because of my time constraints and because I know them to be an excellent networking organization. BIC Recruiting really limited the front-end effort on my end, saving me several days, possibly weeks, of leg work. Further, since BIC really understands the industrial business and has a

215

great network of contacts, it didn't surprise me that the quality of the candidates was very good. They essentially created the 'short list' for me, and arranged a series of back-to-back interviews in the comfort of their office."

Mike Decker, principal of Wingate Partners, on IVS Investment Banking and BIC Alliance:

"IVS Investment Banking and BIC Alliance have the most unique business model. By operating a communications company, they have access to many, many owners in the industrial niche. From advertising and marketing to recruiting and investment banking, they touch the market in so many places. We are thrilled that IVS was able to align us with USA Environment."

Phil Hawk, chairman and CEO of Team Inc./Team Industrial Services, on *Industry Achievers*:

"You have written a very nice chapter on [former Team President and COO] Ken Tholan and I enjoyed reading 'Earl's Pearls of Wisdom' and the '50 Tips for Peace, Happiness and Success.' We should never lose sight of what really matters in life. The book had several good reminders of this throughout."

Paul Tyree, senior vice president, North America, for Total Safety on Earl Heard's Alligator Management & Marketing seminar:

"Earl's seminar was absolutely beneficial to our company. His seminar is realistic, and our salespeople really enjoyed it. The information is practical, and his sales techniques are proven."

216

Works Cited in *Earl's Pearls*

The contributors to this volume referenced the following books, listed alphabetically by author.

The Passion Test, Janet and Chris Attwood

The Business of Listening, Diana Bonet

Good to Great, Jim Collins

The Speed of Trust, Stephen M.R. Covey

Nuts!, Kevin Freiberg and Jackie Freiberg

100 Ways To Bring Out Your Best, Roger Fritz

How to Have Confidence and Power in Dealing With People, Les Giblin

Energy Addict: 101 Physical, Mental, and Spiritual Ways to Energize Your Life, Jon Gordon

The Energy Bus: 10 Rules to Fuel Your Life, Work and Team with Positive Energy, Jon Gordon

Who Moved My Cheese, Spencer Johnson and Kenneth H. Blanchard

The Leadership Challenge, Jim Kouzes and Barry Posner

The Runway of Life, Peter Legge

One Small Step Can Change Your Life, Robert Maurer

Becoming a Person of Influence, John C. Maxwell

Failing Forward, John C. Maxwell

Silent Messages, Albert Mehrabian

Strengths Finder 2.0, Tom Rath

The Fifth Discipline, Peter M. Senge

The Grapes of Wrath, John Steinbeck

Suggested Reading

The Bible, New International Version

How to Read a Book, Mortimer J. Adler and Charles Van Doren

No Such Thing as Impossible, Jairo Alvarez-Botero with Susan D. Mustafa

Dare to Lead: Proven Principles of Effective Leadership, Byrd Baggett

The One Minute Manager, Kenneth Blanchard and Spencer Johnson

The 108 Skills of Natural Born Leaders, Warren Blank

Game Plan: Winning Strategies for the Second Half of Your Life, Bob Buford

Chicken Soup for the Soul, Jack Canfield and Mark Victor Hansen

Sharing Good Times, Jimmy Carter

How to Become a Great Boss, Jeffrey J. Fox

How to Become a Rainmaker, Jeffrey J. Fox

Nuts!: Southwest Airlines' Crazy Recipe for Business and Personal Success, Kevin Freiberg and Jackie Freiberg

The World is Flat, Thomas Friedman

How to Be People Smart, Les Giblin

Outliers, Malcolm Gladwell

The Tipping Point, Malcolm Gladwell

Selling Power's Best, Gerhard Gschwandtner

It's What We Do Together That Counts: The BIC Alliance Story, Earl Heard

Energy Entrepreneurs, Earl Heard and Brady Porche

Industry Achievers, Earl Heard and Brady Porche

Made to Stick: Why Some Ideas Survive and Others Die, Chip Heath and Dan Heath

How to Sell Technical Equipment and Services, James R. Hutton

Anatomy of an Entrepreneur: The Story of Joseph Jacobs, Founder of Jacobs Engineering, Joseph J. Jacobs

Who Moved My Cheese?, Spencer Johnson

How to Wow, Frances Cole Jones

The Power of Tact, Peter Legge

The Guerrilla Marketing Handbook, Jay Levinson and Seth Godin

Wake up, it's Gap-Time, Martha Madden

Messages from God, Lynn Marks

The Long Snapper, Jeffrey Marx

Mentoring 101, John Maxwell

The Entrepreneur's Creed, Merrill Oster and Mike Hamel

Termite, Suzy Pepper

The 22 Immutable Laws of Marketing, Al Ries and Jack Trout

Cain's Redemption, Dennis Shere

The Miracle of Motivation, George Shinn

You Gotta Believe, George Shinn

The Sales Ascent, Kathi Simonsen

Walt Disney: An American Original, Bob Thomas

The Purpose Driven Life, Rick Warren

A Hand to Guide Me, Denzel Washington

101 Winning Tips for Getting a Job, Dr. Shirley White

Dress to Win: 10 Steps to Maximum Personal Impact, Dr. Shirley White

Split Second Choice: The Power of Attitude, Jim Winner

The Prize: The Epic Quest for Oil, Money & Power, Daniel Yergin

Final Thoughts From Earl

America is a nation that consistently recognizes its heroes. It is important to remember, however, that America's heroes are not only in our armed forces, who protect our country, and our firemen and police officers, who protect our lives and our property. America's heroes are also the hardworking people who are on the job every day, keeping business and industry moving.

Just as our brothers in the agricultural, retail and health care industries help keep us fed, clothed and healthy, it is those of us in the energy, construction, and oil and gas industries who keep the nation's wheels turning and its lights burning, who help build and maintain America's homes, commercial buildings and industrial facilities.

But, friends, keeping America strong is more than building a strong economy and maintaining a powerful military. It is also how we teach and train our youth and those members of our work forces who will become tomorrow's leaders.

Just as our schoolteachers across the land partner with us and teach our children and grandchildren the Three R's — readin', 'ritin' and 'rythmetic — we must become partners with tomorrow's leaders and help instill within them a sense of character, honor, integrity, respect, and, of course, knowledge of the jobs they must perform.

The latter is one of the many ways that BIC Alliance is helping build a stronger America. By disseminating the knowledge that not only our staff has garnered, but the experience and expertise of our marketing partners and *BIC Magazine* readers, we are in our own way helping pass the torch from one generation to the next.

We very much appreciate the help that all of you have given us over the years, submitting articles, sharing your knowledge, helping us build the America to be on the America that was and is.

And, never has the need for teaching and training been more crucial than today. In recent years, many industry leaders with decades of experience in honorable traditions have either passed away, retired or been laid off during cutbacks. Add that to an aging work force, and you can easily see how critical it is that the knowledge amassed during decades of industry be passed along to the next generation.

The absolute necessity of training was brought home to me several years ago when my granddaughter, Hannah, was about to undertake her first cookie sale with her Brownie troop. My daughter and son-in-law, Dane and Thomas, were sharing with Hannah and her troop tips on how to sell more cookies. Thomas and Dane didn't just tell Hannah and her fellow Brownies how to do it, they actually demonstrated a sale and coached the girls on proper procedure.

As Hannah learned the intricacies of the selling process, she became more excited and anxious to employ her newly developed skills.

I sincerely believe that our leaders of tomorrow (our children, grandchildren and protégés) are just as anxious and excited to learn and to use the knowledge they gain in their daily lives.

I also feel that those of us who have accumulated that experience and knowledge should be just as excited to pass it on, just as we should have that thrilling sense of expectation at the opportunity to learn new and varied things.

Quite often, however, it seems that younger folks are more willing and anxious to learn than some of the old timers who think they may already know it all. The fact is, we never get too old or have too much experience to learn from others.

In today's changing work place, it is not at all unusual to find young managers who oversee people who may be older and more experienced than they. What many people fail to realize is that no matter if it is a seasoned veteran supervisor training a younger person, or someone younger who manages older and more experienced people, the concept those supervisors have grasped is that the key to success is in establishing partnering relationships built on empathy and mutual respect.

It should also be noted that those partnering relationships need not necessarily be created by those seeking the same goal. In management and marketing, for example, we need to build relationships with folks whose agenda is not the same as ours, but with whom by working together we can each achieve our goals.

Unfortunately, folks sometimes approach these situations thinking only of themselves, never realizing the value of working in tandem. They don't accept the concept of sharing expertise or working together for the betterment of all. Now, perhaps more than ever, that is a very self-defeating attitude.

Instead of becoming aggravated or disheartened, cooler heads must prevail, and we must demonstrate a true concern for others and show patience for them. We must rely on our people skills to turn potential adversaries into allies.

This is, of course, much easier said than done. But, for those who can accomplish it, this is the mark of a true professional, regardless of one's age. For those of us who can achieve such skill in dealing with others, it is one of the most vital aspects of our knowledge that we can pass along in our teaching and training.

It is important to remember that we should always share our pearls of wisdom with others. If you'd like to share some with us for possible inclusion in a future book, send them to Brady Porche at brady@bicalliance.com.

226

228